SUBSTANCE ABUSE

SUBSTANCE ABUSE

Pharmacologic and
Developmental Perspectives

PURCELL TAYLOR, Jr.
B.A., M.Ed., Ed.D., C.C.D.C., Q.M.R.P.

Certified Chemical Dependency Counselor
Evaluator Case Presentation Method (CPM)
Certified School Psychologist
Associate Professor of Psychology
University College
University of Cincinnati

and

Former Adjunct Associate Professor of School Psychology
Department of School Psychology and Counseling
University of Cincinnati

and

Broadview Developmental Center Superintendent
Ohio Department of Mental Retardation and
Developmental Disabilities

Property of
LIBRARY
MITCHELL COMMUNITY COLLEGE
STATESVILLE, NC 28677 *37,033*

CHARLES C THOMAS · PUBLISHER
Springfield · Illinois · U.S.A.

Published and Distributed Throughout the World by

CHARLES C THOMAS • PUBLISHER

2600 South First Street

Springfield, Illinois 62794-9265

© *1988 by* CHARLES C THOMAS • PUBLISHER

ISBN 0-398-05484-3

Library of Congress Catalog Card Number: 88-8587

Printed in the United States of America
Q-R-3

Library of Congress Cataloging in Publication Data

Taylor, Purcell.
    Substance abuse.
    Includes bibliographies and index.
    1. Substance abuse. 2. Psychopharmacology.
I. Title. [DNLM: 1. Psychopharmacology. 2. Sub-
stance Abuse. WM 270 T245s]
RC564.T39   1988   616.86   88-8587
ISBN 0-398-05484-3

I am deeply grateful to Dr. J.F. Bonfiglio for his unselfish support and assistance in my development as a drug specialist.

ACKNOWLEDGMENTS

I WISH TO acknowledge the work of those pioneers, many of whom are mentioned in this volume, who contributed to the advancement of drug abuse. Certainly it is impossible to give credit to everyone who enlightened the scientific drug abuse community to this field.

I wish to thank the publisher, Charles Thomas, Publisher, for their confidence in the merits of my efforts.

I am also grateful to the many students whom I have taught at the undergraduate and graduate levels as well as clients; both gave me many penetrating insights into developing a textbook of interest to students, clinicians and researchers.

Finally, I wish to acknowledge the efforts of Barbara A. Ish and Lunette J. Baldwin, who spent many months on the typing and preparation of the manuscript.

I trust the reader will realize that numerous gaps in our present knowledge of drug abuse still exist, but hope that future researchers will build on this model.

CONTENTS

SUBSTANCE ABUSE

Chapter 1

DRUG ABUSE, AN OVERVIEW

DRUG ABUSE in the United States is a major health problem that exerts a heavy toll from our society in terms of economic costs and human suffering. Society's difficulty with drug abuse has been attributed to an unwillingness to recognize the distinction between the concept of illicit drug use and the realities of hard-core abuse. In addition, most individuals fail to recognize the extent to which attitudes and values are involved in the drug abuse issue, or they tend to react on the basis of feelings rather than fact.

Without a doubt, the decade of the eighties is the decade of polydrug abuse. Listen to the rock music! Eighty-five percent of all alcoholics and drug abusers, both young and old, are polydrug users or abusers, but not necessarily addicts (Talbott, 1982). The decade of the eighties is the age of sedativism and polydrug use and our society is paying the price. A recent study by Research Triangle Institute (RTI) has estimated that the minimal cost of drug abuse to the American economy in 1977 alone was over sixteen billion dollars. Of this amount, young males (ages 18-24) paid a high penalty, with more than three billion dollars due to lost employment and reduced productivity. Admittedly, these estimates are quite conservative (Federal Strategy for Prevention of Drug Abuse and Drug Trafficking, 1982.)

Economic costs incurred by society overall were defined by the disease-oriented model as to cost of health care, cost of security and the criminal justice system, losses in productivity due to morbidity, premature mortality, incarceration, or involvement in criminal activity. However, the RTI study did not include the economic costs to society for consumer expenditures for illicit drugs, the transfer of illicit drug monies from the United States to other countries. Nor did it consider the cost

3

to the individual of violent or property crime associated with drug abuse (Federal Strategy for Prevention of Drug Abuse and Drug Trafficking, 1982).

Finally, there is some difficulty as one might well imagine in placing a dollar value on the pain, suffering, and family disruption that is often seen with substance abuse. However, the costs are well understood by those individuals affected.

It certainly makes little difference whether we are talking about heroinism, quaaludism, amphetaminism, cocainism, alcoholism, demerolism, or dilaudism, because we are referring to addictive mood-altering drugs that cost our society tremendously in human and economic terms.

We are a drug-oriented society. For example, we often hear someone saying "mother needs something to wake up in the morning, to stay on her diet, and something to relax her during the day." Truly the phrase, "Better living through chemistry," has become a reality. As a society, we consume a host of different drugs for a variety of purposes. Our society spends an incredible amount of money each year for legal chemicals that alter mood or consciousness.

The 33rd Annual Report on Consumer Spending (1979 and 1980) reported total spending in the following classes of legal chemicals: (1) Over-The-Counter (OTC) Drugs — 3.4 billion, including cough and cold items, external and internal analgesics, antacids, laxatives, sleep aids, and sedatives, (2) Social Drugs — 50.9 billion for alcohol, 21.7 billion for tobacco, and 5.0 billion for coffee, tea, and cocoa, (3) Prescription, or ethical drugs — 12.7 billion, and (4) Miscellaneous drugs, aerosols, nutmeg, and others — the amount here is undetermined.

With regard to illegal drugs, Americans spend hundreds of billions of dollars each year. For example, it is estimated that cocaine alone generates approximately one hundred billion dollars each year.

Current levels of drug abuse are strikingly higher than in earlier times. There are thousands of individuals who are addicted to narcotics; between 2 and 2.5 million individuals chronically use barbiturates and other sedatives. As many as 5 million people take illegally obtained oral amphetamines. On the other hand, a downward trend has been observed in the use of both hallucinogens and heroin nationwide (National Institute on Drug Abuse (NIDA), 1981).

USE AND ABUSE

There is a distinction between the use and the abuse of drugs. In today's society it would be more difficult to find someone who has not used a psychoactive substance than to find someone who has used a psychoactive substance. However, not everyone misuses or abuses these drugs. Misusing a drug simply means using the drug in a manner that can have detrimental psychological or physiological effects. Becoming drunk may be considered by some a misuse of alcohol, however, it does not necessarily follow that the drunk person is an alcoholic with symptoms. There are many definitions of drug abuse. The National Institute on Drug Abuse (NIDA) defines drug abuse as use that results in the physical, mental, emotional, or social impairment of the user. However, the author prefers to define drug abuse as a cognitive cortical, cultural bad habit which poses a serious threat to health or to psychological and social functioning. Others, such as the Jehovah Witnesses, Mormons, or Christian Scientists, would consider even the use of alcohol and coffee as abusive. Probably few would agree on what defines what is excessive or dangerous with regard to use or abuse. Generally, the public and the law have defined the recreational use of any illicit psychoactive substance as abuse without any demonstration of individual harm or social consequences necessary.

ADDICTION: The term addiction comes from the Latin verb *addicere*: to give or bind a person to one thing or another. Generally, the term addiction is used in the drug field to refer to chronic compulsivity, loss of control, and continued use despite negative consequences (Smith, 1982). Beyond this, the term is ambiguously used with a wide variety of often arbitrary meanings and connotations; sometimes interchangeably with, sometimes in contrast to, two other ill-defined terms, habituation and drug dependence. Habituation imprecisely refers to some lesser form of chronic drug use, while drug dependency refers to the capability of being psychological or physical in origin, often in varying combinations depending on the drug used (NIDA, 1982).

DRUG ABUSE THEORIES

INTRAPERSONAL PSYCHOLOGICAL TRAITS

There is a considerable amount of literature concerning drug abuse and personality. However helpful these studies may be, they are largely irrelevant from the point of view of drug abuse etiology.

Intrapersonal or trait theories hold the view that the individual is the carrier of certain psychological traits or predispositions that may operate or exist independently of the presence or actions of others. However, this is not to deny the importance of social interaction in either the genesis or expression of such traits (Nurco, 1981).

It is important to recognize that the vast majority of theories having relevance to the etiology of drug abuse are primarily intrapersonal. Consequently, a wide variety of psychological instruments have been proposed for assessing drug use and abuse. Perhaps, the most widely used instrument for the purposes of measuring personality traits concerning drug abuse is the Minnesota Multiphasic Personality Inventory (MMPI) (Hathaway and McKinley, 1967). Additionally, other inventories have been used for assessing intrapersonal traits such as the Sixteen Personality Factor questionnaire (16 PF) (Cattell and Eber, 1961), California Psychological Inventory (CPI) (Gough, 1957), Eysenck Personality Inventory (EPI) (Eysenck and Eysenck, 1964), and the Addiction Research Center Inventory (ARCI) (Haertzen and Hill, 1963).

Concerning the MMPI, the typical addictive personality pattern that emerges is usually interpreted as one of psychopathic or antisocial personality as indicated by primary peaks on the **PD** (Psychopathic Deviate-Scale 4) and **MA** (Hypomania-Scale 9) scales.

Secondary peaks on **SC** (Schizophrenia-Scale 8) and **D** (Depression-Scale 2) are sometimes noted as well, but elevations on the latter are frequently a function of current circumstances (e.g., economic conditions, incarceration, treatment status, etc.). On the other hand, scales 4 and 9 are thought to tap more enduring, characterological traits, and for this reason they are frequently regarded as revealing the essence of any trait commonalities among addicts in general.

On the CPI, addicts seem to score low on measures of responsibility and socialization (Haertzen, 1978). With respect to the 16PF, there is evidence that addicts as a group significantly exceed the standardization norms on Scale C (emotionally unstable), Scale L (suspecting and jealous), Scale M (eccentric and unconcerned), and Scale O (insecure and anxious). These characterizations are both internally consistent and in keeping with clinical formulations and observations made over the years by numerous investigators in the field of drug abuse (Nurco, 1979).

IMMEDIATE GRATIFICATION HYPOTHESIS

In the field of drug abuse, it is commonly observed that some individuals have a great difficulty in deferring gratification. Deferring gratification seems to be an important factor in the life styles of addicts.

Several investigators have suggested a conceptual basis for the emergence of this trait. "Delays in satisfaction constitute dangers to early infantile survival and as such are sources of augmented tension referred to as fear" (Sullivan, 1953). Addicts appear to behave as if the tensions of unfulfilled wants creates an unbearable situation. Waiting becomes unbearable because future gratification cannot be guaranteed. In addition, addicts and other deviant groups appear to have an inability to trust persons in authority. It has also been suggested that preference for delayed rather than immediate reward may be associated with significant differences in maturity, social responsibility, long-term goal direction, autonomy, and father's presence during the formative years (Mischel, 1961).

THE BOREDOM-RELIEF HYPOTHESIS

The boredom-relief model invokes the concept of boredom. Many individuals experience extreme boredom, which can lead to both depression and an inability to function. One mechanism for combating boredom is the frantic pursuit of almost any activity. Applied to narcotic addiction, such a mechanism provides a double reinforcement. In seeking narcotics, the addict runs about filling up his/her day with "taking care of business" and thus alleviating boredom with these activities. Afterwards, the drug experience itself removes the boredom and the cycle is further strengthened and repeated.

WHY DO PEOPLE TAKE DRUGS

Since antiquity, both civilized and primitive people have used a near infinite number of chemical substances for such purposes as seeking pleasure, pursuing divine insight, escapism, and increasing aggression or strength, as well as the socially acceptable purposes of preventing or treating diseases. However, drug abuse is unknown in primitive societies because they do not use drugs for purposes of escape. Instead, drugs have been used in these societies to strengthen cultural values and goals. Further, drug use is controlled in these societies by ritual rather than by legal means. Additionally, drugs are used under the guidance of usually a shaman who employs music or odors to evoke specific kinds of visions. In these societies, psychoactive drugs are used to support healing, to forecast the future course of a disease, and to protect the community from its enemies. Primitive societies rarely used drugs to reduce anxiety or to escape personal problems.

The use of psychoactive drugs can be seen as an alternative for formal coping skills in handling subjective needs and problems. The use of drugs, whether inside or outside the medical system, is a matter of personal choice. Individuals use or abuse drugs that fit their particular needs or that are deemed desirable by some significant reference group. The motivation for the use of any drug depends on the individual's needs and problems. Consequently, drugs serve a variety of functions for the individual and these functions may vary at different periods in the user's life. For example, individuals may be attracted to particular pharmacologic properties of drugs to produce positive feelings or reduce pain. Some individuals use drugs as a rationalization for openly acting out in ways not acceptable to individuals or society. Drugs like marijuana and alcohol, that disinhibit, could serve such a licensing function. Drug use may also be associated with a secondary gain not directly connected to the pharmacological effects. The individual may simply be seeking to obtain or maintain companionship, status, or identity. Finally, certain functions have to do with a prior expectation about drug effects and therefore become symbolic (NIDA, 1982). Drug use may be a means of expressing hostility, understanding consciousness and perceiving deeper truths, gaining status in some reference group, and expressing civil disobedience in issues of principle.

CHILD AND ADOLESCENT DRUG ABUSE

The use of psychoactive drugs by young people is a widespread and growing problem. National studies show that more of today's teenagers are beginning to use alcohol at earlier ages than the youth of 30 or 40 years ago, and they are getting drunk more frequently. Approximately 95 percent of our country's teens have tried alcohol, compared to an average of 53 percent of their counterparts in the 1940's and 1950's. Today's young drinkers may add drugs, such as marijuana, to their drinking habit. And by the end of their school years, 60 percent have tried marijuana. In addition, this trend is seen to hold for other drugs as well.

About a third of teenage Americans have their first drink before age 14, and an estimated 27 percent of high school students drink at least once a week. The consequences are often tragic. It is estimated that between 40 and 50 percent of fatal automobile crashes involving young people are alcohol-related and 8,000 or more teenagers are killed each year in automobile accidents. Although adolescent alcohol and drug use is often experimental, recreational, or short-term, there is a small but increasing adolescent population whose drug use is more alarming.

In Wisconsin, for example, approximately 10 percent of the state's population 12 years of age and over are alcoholics and alcohol abusers. Also, this statistic includes an estimated 80,667 problem drinkers ages 12 to 20.

Additionally, when we consider other drugs such as cigarettes, most of the initial experiences took place before high school. For example, 15 percent began daily cigarette smoking prior to tenth grade vs. only an additional 9 percent in high school (i.e., in grades ten through twelve).

Among inhalant users (unadjusted for nitrite underreporting), over half had their first experience prior to tenth grade. However, this unadjusted statistic probably reflects the predominant pattern for such inhalants as glues and aerosols, which tend to be used primarily at younger ages.

PCP use shows a relatively early age of initiation as well, with about 40 percent of the eventual users having started before high school.

For each illicit drug except inhalants and marijuana, less than half of the users had begun use prior to tenth grade. Among those who used cocaine by senior year, only about one in seven had used it prior to tenth grade. For most of the other illicit drugs, the corresponding proportion is roughly from one-fifth to one-third. These data do indicate that significant minorities of eventual users of these drugs are initiated into drug use prior to tenth grade (NIDA, 1982).

Adolescence is a period of particular vulnerability to drug abuse. During this period of transition from childhood to adulthood, the adolescent has no real status in our society. The adolescent is constantly struggling to achieve an identity and new ways to handle stress. For some adolescents, the "high" gained from chemicals offers temporary relief from the pressures and anxiety associated with this stage of life. Additionally, it helps the adolescent to cope, reduce stress, and find a group of drinking and drug-using peers.

The chronic use and subsequent dependency on chemicals interferes with the adolescent's development of a positive self-image and the appropriate use of leisure time. Adolescent drug abuse may not always reach the point of addiction. However, the psychological effects and associated problems in the areas of health, family relationships, education, and career development may reach disastrous proportions. Particularly when it comes to alcohol and drug abuse problems, the adolescent has unique needs. Recognizing these needs and providing specialized services to adolescents is a major public health concern.

WOMEN AND DRUG ABUSE

Recently, women have been receiving increasing attention with respect to their drug abuse and their involvement in drug treatment programs. (Burt, Glynn, and Sowder, 1979). However, little substantive knowledge exists regarding the epidemiology of substance abuse among women because women tend to receive attention in the literature mainly when there is concern about their effect on family members and others. Thus, this outlook reflects the traditional American sex roles centering around the familiar division of labor (Celentano, McQueen, and Chess, 1980). Over half of the patients treated in hospital emergency rooms for drug-related episodes in 1980 were women. Although only 28 percent of the clients admitted to federally funded drug treatment facilities in 1980 were women, they represented significant portions of the clients in some drug categories. Women, for example, represent 51 percent of all persons treated in federal treatment programs for tranquilizer abuse, 38 percent of persons treated for abuse of other sedatives, 35 percent of persons treated for amphetamine abuse, 34 percent of persons treated for barbiturate abuse, and 33 percent of persons treated for abuse of opiates other than heroin (NIDA, 1983). The proportion of each sex using any illicit drug suggests that use has been declining among males since 1978 (from 59% to 54% in 1981) while increasing slightly among females (from 49% in 1978 to 51% in 1981); that between 1978 and 1981 lifetime amphetamine use by females rose by 10 percent (from 23% to 33%) while use by males rose by 8 percent (from 22% to 30%).

In addition, women receive 60 percent of the prescriptions for all drugs and 67 percent of the prescriptions for psychoactive drugs. Women are also much more likely than men to obtain psychoactive drugs from a physician; men tend to obtain them from less legitimate sources. Obtaining psychoactive drugs from a physician rather than from other sources has been shown to lead to longer and more consistent drug use (Prather, 1975).

In the last decade, the use of heroin among women has increased more rapidly than among men and about 20 percent of all known addicts are women. The average female heroin addict is white and from a blue-collar background. These women report negative relationships with their fathers. They frequently lack high school educations, are currently or formerly married, and engage in prostitution or other illegal activities to support their habits (Prather, 1978). The female user tends to become involved with narcotics in her mid-twenties, after introduction to drugs by a male companion. In contrast to men, women tend to use a variety of drugs, rather than just heroin (NIDA, 1983, Prather, 1978). Overuse of these drugs has led to increasing rates of suicide among women and they are the most frequent suicide method used by women. Psychoactive drug abuse in women is attributed to society's encouragement of women to express emotional stress and to alleviate it with drugs. Treatment for such women is frequently inadequate. They often do not receive birth control counseling, special health care for pregnancy, or child care services at treatment centers. Job training, career counseling, and job placement are also insufficient, and treatment staff are male-oriented and may be sexually abusive. In comparison to men, fewer women enter some type of treatment program. Women also have lower retention rates and experience a lower level of success whenever they do enter treatment.

MINORITIES AND DRUG ABUSE

As a racially oppressed minority in America, blacks are presumably exposed to greater degrees of psychosocial and other stresses than white Americans (Arsenian and Arsenian, 1948). The critical stressor for the black American is economic. Poor economic conditions lead to circumstances such as poor housing, poor education, poor nutrition, less than adequate medical care, crime, and low self-esteem. Even when legitimate jobs open to many ghetto residents, especially young black males, they pay low wages, are demeaning, and carry the risk of lay-offs.

As a result, drug use not only makes life more tolerable for slum dwellers but provides companionship and an identity. In addition, some slum dwellers turn to crime such as drug-dealing because of its few technological requirements, minimal educational demands, and high profits. Historically, crime has served as an elusive symbol of success and upward mobility for the poor. Thus, participation in this subeconomy provides minorities at best with a marginal income (Yeager, 1975). The attraction of this activity remains strong in certain communities because of the visible success of selected entrepreneurs, particularly in the sale of illicit drugs. Consequently, the reinforcement from the sale of illicit drugs is encouraged by profitability and the insatiable public demand for the drug experience. Therefore, ethnic minority participation in this irregular economy represents a rational adaptation on their part to avail themselves to this economic opportunity. Clearly, one should recognize that such sociodemographic factors play a role in the development of substance abuse among minorities. However, one should not lose sight of the fact that the vast majority of minorities in dire socioeconomic circumstances do not pursue careers in drug abuse (Nurco, 1981).

Donald Freeman of Community Research, Inc. (Washington) testified about the drug situation in the black community "For minorities in general and Blacks in particular, the anxieties produced by oppression often leads us to reach out for the most immediate alleviator which most often turns out to be a chemical escape...All of these realities and more make Black people more subject to the use of chemicals to temporarily escape this oppression and consequently more vulnerable to an increase in the availability of dangerous drugs. All drug policy that tends to increase the availability of drugs in our communities should be actively opposed" (Freeman, 1976).

Historical examples in the recent past and in other settings as well shed light on this issue. For example, after the riots in Los Angeles and following the assassination of Dr. Martin Luther King, Jr., an unusually large amount of heroin was made available on the streets of the Black communities. The purpose was clear: someone "high on smack" can't fight back. (Smith, 1977.)

In a society where personal racism and institutionalized racism are so widespread and deeply rooted, is it any wonder that deadly drugs are preferentially sold in nonwhite neighborhoods? Under conditions of high unemployment and labor unrest, is it any wonder that deadly drugs are preferentially sold to unemployed and frustrated workers? The drug industry has no "code of ethics" it will use anyone who will pay the price.

HEALTH PROFESSIONALS AND DRUG ABUSE

Contrary to what the general public may wish to believe about its health care providers, problems of alcoholism and other drug dependency syndromes do exist. However, numerous treatment programs for health care providers have been established throughout the United States (Talbott, 1976, 1982). For obvious reasons, it is difficult for the general public to accept that a health professional who is dedicated to the preservation and restoration of health could be vulnerable to problems of substance abuse. Even more difficult is for health professionals to accept substance abuse problems in themselves as well as in their peers. Recently, it has become evident that anyone in the health care field is at risk for developing a substance abuse problem.

Traditionally, nurses, psychologists, psychiatrists, physicians, pharmacists, pharmacy technicians, dentists, and veterinarians have been included among the professionals at risk of developing a substance abuse problem. The reason for these particular groups being recognized is that they are involved in prescribing, dispensing, or administrating drugs. Other professionals not directly involved in drug delivery but who provide health care services are also at risk since their attitudes are similar to the professionals mentioned above in the delivery of health services.

Currently, few studies give any reliable estimates of the number of substance abusers who are health care professionals (Canfield, 1976). However, the health care professionals are as likely as the general public to become alcoholic but are more likely to become involved in the abuse of prescription drugs (Isler, 1978; Johnson and Keenly, 1981; Vaillant, 1970). The risk of the development of the disease of chemical dependency has been estimated to be 15-20 percent among the health care providers (Canfield, 1976).

Recognition and treatment of the impaired health care professional is important to protect the public as well as assist the addict. Treatment approaches for the health care professional range from separate facilities, total integration programs, to combination programs. Our knowledge of chemical dependency can help in the early intervention of the addictive cycle so that reentry may be less stressful.

ARMED FORCES AND DRUG ABUSE

Drug abuse by members of the Armed Forces is a continuing problem which increases the cost of maintaining appropriate levels of readiness. The majority of military drug abusers are male, single, and under the age of twenty-five. The twenty-five year age represents 63 percent of the Armed Forces of the United States. As is found in the general population, the most common substances of abuse are alcohol and marijuana. Two out of three in the enlisted grades E1 to E5 indicate that they are using alcohol or marijuana at least once a month.

Current available evidence indicates that addiction and serious psychopathology, although present in relatively small percentages of abusers, does not present a major problem in the military. Rather, the problems with drugs and alcohol are quite similar to those found in civilian populations within the same age group. The prevention of drug abuse in the military has become an urgent concern for those in leadership roles. Those in leadership have come to recognize that even low levels of drug use and abuse present our country with great potential for harm and national hazard.

Therefore, the Department of Defense has recently established a goal of a drug-free military. Since drug abuse is incompatible with the maintenance of high standards of military readiness and discipline, maintaining a high standard of preparedness requires a reliable and sensitive system of drug monitoring, assessment, incentives for servicemen and women. Additionally, there is a need for effective treatment programs, carefully drawn policies regarding penalties for illicit drug use designed primarily to return military personnel to active duty as a fully functioning member of the Armed Forces of the United States.

ELDERLY AND DRUG ABUSE

Understanding the abuse or misuse of drugs by the elderly has become an area of increasing concern to the drug abuse field (NIDA, 1982).

In 1975, the National Institute on Drug Abuse awarded a grant to the Department of Sociology, University of Houston, for research on the use of psychoactive substances by the elderly and the problems associated with such use.

The results of the study indicates that the use of psychoactive substances does not pose a major public health problem to persons aged 55 and older. The study showed, within its ability to generalize, that less than a fifth of the sample currently used any psychoactive drugs and that only a little over half reported having ever used a psychoactive substance in their lifetime. These data were remarkably similar to data reported by other researchers.

If misuse is defined as failure to follow prescription direction, almost 40 percent of the users had failed at least once to follow prescription directions. However, the vast bulk of these persons (86.8%) reported that they took less drug than directed. While this can have important clinical implications for some disorders (e.g., organic brain syndrome), for most psychoactive substances, medication error was probably in the safe direction. Moreover, less than 1 percent of the total sample reported themselves as taking more of a psychoactive drug than was prescribed. In short, noncompliance with physician prescription was far more likely to be in the direction of avoiding drug effects than of seeking those effects.

Less than 2 percent reported any lifetime use of an illicit drug. Indeed, only about 40 percent of the sample had drunk any alcoholic beverages in the month preceding the interview, and only 17.7 percent reported drinking an alcoholic beverage on the day before being inter-viewed. Only 5.7 percent of the total sample reported themselves as hav-ing currently used both psychoactive substance and alcohol. In short, the ambulatory elderly appear to be responsible consumers of psychoac-tive substances (NIDA, 1982).

CUES FOR DRUG ABUSE IDENTIFICATION

Although drug abuse in its different forms can produce recognizable effects, almost all such manifestations are, at their onset, identical to those produced by conditions not related to drug abuse.

A clue to the possibility of drug abuse comes with persistence of symptoms which might otherwise appear "routine." Whenever tablets, capsules, or other forms of drugs are found on a person suspected of be-ing an abuser, they may not necessarily be narcotics or any other dangerous drug.

There are no instant tests for drug identification. The only sure way to identify most drugs is through a series of laborious laboratory proce-dures conducted by trained professionals, because many drugs are iden-tical in their appearance. Generally, there are signs which may suggest drug abuse (including the following):

1. Sudden and dramatic changes in discipline.
2. Job performance decreases.
3. Display of an unusual degree of activity or inactivity.
4. Sudden and irrational flareups involving strong emotions and/or tempers.
5. Worsening of personal appearance.
6. Furtive behavior regarding actions and possessions.
7. Sunglasses worn at inappropriate times and places.
8. Wearing of long-sleeve garments constantly, even in very hot weather (hide track marks).
9. Association with known drug abusers or addicts.
10. Trying to borrow money from several individuals (purchase drugs).
11. Stealing of such items as cameras, radios, jewelry, etc. to convert to cash and buy drugs.
12. At odd times may be found in such places as storage rooms or closets.

In addition to the signs above, there are more specific symptoms which are consistent with specific classes of drug abusers.

1. CNS Depressant — Drugs such as the barbiturates and certain tranquilizers, exhibit most of the symptoms of alcohol intoxication with one exception — no odor of alcohol on breath. Individuals taking these drugs often stagger and stumble, and may fall into a deep sleep. Finally, these individuals lack interest in activities, are drowsy, and appear disoriented.

2. Stimulants — Those using this class of drugs (e.g., amphetamine) display excessive activities. The abuser is irritable, argumentative, appears extremely nervous, and has difficulty sitting. Sometimes the pupils of the eyes may dilate even in bright light.

Drugs like amphetamine cause a drying effect on the mucous membranes of the mouth, nose with resultant bad breath that is unidentifiable as to specific odor such as onion, garlic, or alcohol. Due to the dryness of the mouth, the abuser licks his/her lips to keep them moist. Consequently, this leads to chapped, reddened lips. In severe cases, the lips are raw and may crack and bleed.

Dryness of the mucuous membrane in the nose is also seen in those who abuse the stimulant drugs. Dryness in this instance causes the abuser to rub and scratch his/her nose vigorously and frequently to relieve the itching sensation. Finally, the stimulant abuser may go long periods of time without sleeping or eating, and cannot resist letting others know about it.

3. Hallucinogens — Individuals abusing the hallucinogens usually sit or recline quietly in a dream or trance-like state. On occasion, the user becomes fearful and experiences a degree of terror which may cause them to attempt to flee their surroundings.

4. Narcotics — Appears lethargic, drowsy, or seems intoxicated. The pupils of the eyes are often constricted and fail to respond to light.

Some abusers inhale narcotic drugs such as heroin in its powder form. Afterwards, small traces of white powder can be seen around the nostrils of the user. The frequent inhalation of these drugs causes the nose to redden and become raw. Most often, the narcotic is injected directly into the blood vessel. After repeated injections, the inner surface of the arm at the elbow develops scars or "track marks." Consequently, the identification of these track marks causes the narcotic abuser to wear long sleeve garments at odd times. Many female narcotic abusers use makeup to cover up their scars. Finally, associated with narcotic injections are diseases caused by unsterile conditions such as hepatitis, blood poisoning, and AIDS.

As indicated above, we are a drug oriented society. However, if we as a society are to be effective at any level of drug abuse prevention or treatment, the individual must be allowed to maintain his or her integrity—a difficult task for any complex society. To criticize weaknesses (psychopathology) in the drug user and not criticize the weaknesses in a society that causes drug abuse (economic, racial, employment) only worsens the situation. Drug abuse is a disease of society as well as the individual. Let us not give in to a defeatist impulse. It is no longer a question of right or wrong, it is now a question of **survival**.

REFERENCES

Arsenian, J., and Arsenian, J.M. Tough and Easy Cultures; A Conceptual Analysis, *Psychiatry*, 11:377-385, 1948.

Burt, M.R., Glynn, T.J., and Sowder, B.J. *Psychological Characteristics of Drug-Abusing Women*, National Institution on Drug Abuse, DHEW Pub. No. (ADM), Services Research Monograph, Washington, D.C.: Supt. of Docs., U.S. Govt. Print. Off., 80-917, 1979.

Canfield, T.M. Drug Addiction of Health Professionals, *AORN Journal*, 24(4):665-671, 1976.

Cattell, R.B., and Eber, H. *The 16 Personality Factor Questionnaire*, (3rd Edition), Champaign, IL: Institute for Personality and Ability Testing, 1961.

Celentano, D.D., McQueen, D.V., and Chess, E. Substance Abuse by Women: A Review of the Epidemiologic Literature, *Journal of Chronic Diseases*, 33(6):383-394, 1980.

Dahlstrom, W. Grant, Welsh, George Schlager, and Dahlstrom, Leona E. An MMPI Handbook, Vol. 1, *Clinical Interpretation*, Revised (1982).

Drug Taking Among the Elderly, U.S. Department of Health and Human Services; Alcohol, Drug Abuse, and Mental Health Administration, U.S. Printing Office, 1982.

Eysenck, H.J., and Eysenck, S.B.G. *Manual of the Eysenck Personality Inventory*, London: University of London Press, 1964.

Federal Strategy for Prevention of Drug Abuse and Drug Trafficking, U.S. Government Printing Office, Washington, D.C., 20402, 1982.

Freeman, Donald. *Proceedings of the National Hearing of the Heroin Epidemic*, sponsored by The Program to Combat Drug Abuse, United Church of Christ, held in the Cannon Office Building (Washington, D.C.), June 29, 1976.

Gough, H.G. *California Psychological Inventory Manual*, Palo Alto, CA: Consulting Psychologists Press, 1957.

Haertzen, C.A. Historical View of Characteristics of Addicts, In W.R. Martin and H. Isbell (Eds.), *Drug Addiction and the U.S. Public Health Service. Proceeding of Symposium Commemorating the Fortieth Anniversary of Addiction Research Center at Lexington, Ky.*, Rockville, MD: DHEW Pub. (AMD), 77-434, 1978.

Haertzen, C.A., and Hill, H.E. Assessing Subjective Effects of Drugs: An Index of Carelessness and Confusion for Use With the Addiction Research Center Inventory (ARCI), *Journal of Clinical Psychology*, 19-407-412, 1963.

Hathaway, S.R., and McKinley, J.C. *The MMPI Manual*: The Psychological Corporation, 1951; Revised 1967.

Isler, C. The Alcoholic Nurse: What We Try To Deny, *RN*, 41(7):48-55, 1978.

Johnson, R.P., and Keenly, J.C. Addicted Physicians—A Closer Look, *Journal of the American Medical Association*, 245(3):253-257, 1981.

Mischel, W. Father Absence and Delay of Gratification: A Crosscultural Comparison, *Journal of Abnormal and Social Psychology*, 63:116-124, 1961.

Nurco, D.H. Etiological Aspects of Drug Abuse, In R.L. DuPont, A. Goldstein, and J. O'Donnell (Eds.), *Handbook of Drug Abuse*, Washington, D.C.: U.S. Government Printing Office, 1979.

Nurco, David H. Precursors of Addiction, Research Monograph Series, *Problems of Drug Dependence*, National Institute of Drug Abuse, 1981.

Prather, J., and Fidell, L.S. Sex Differences in the Content and Style of Medical Advertisements, *Social Science & Medicine*, 9(1):23-26, 1975.

Prather, J.E., and Fidell, L.S. Drug Abuse and Abuse Among Women: An Overview. *The International Journal of the Addictions*, 13(6):863-885, 1978.

Research Issues 31: Women and Drugs, National Institute on Drug Abuse, U.S. Department of Health and Human Services, 1983.

Smith, David. National Symposium on Psychiatry/Chemical Dependence, Atlanta, GA, 1982.

Chapter 2

THE CENTRAL AND AUTONOMIC SYSTEMS

IN AN ANIMAL with an intact vertebral (spinal column), there are two chief parts of the nervous system. Anatomically, they are the central nervous system (CNS) and the peripheral nervous system (PNS). The central nervous system consists of the brain and the spinal cord. The CNS is responsible for the interpretation of and reaction to all information that the body receives from the environment. The second portion of the nervous system is called the peripheral nervous system (PNS). This system is made up of nerve fibers that conduct information toward the CNS (afferent fibers) and nerve fibers that conduct directives from the CNS to all other body areas (efferent fibers) (Taylor, 1982).

THE NEURON

The brain is composed of billions of neurons, or nerve cells, located mainly within the cranial cavity. The neuron is considered the base of all activities of the nervous system.

Neurons differ from other body cells in two ways: (1) They are specialized to respond to electrical, chemical, and physical changes over long distances and (2) They function to transmit impulses to other innervated tissue in a highly specialized manner.

The neuron consists of : (1) **Dendrites**, which carry information to the cell body, (2) **Cell Body**, the site of the synthesis for synthetic and degradative enzymes and for storage vesicles. Also, precursors are taken up into the cell from the surrounding environment by a specific uptake mechanism, (3) **Axon**, transport enzymes, vesicles, and precursors from the cell body to the nerve terminals. Some axons are covered by a fatty layer of tissue called the **Myelin Sheath**. (Fig. 2.0). In addition, the neuron conducts electrical impulses of nervous transmission. The

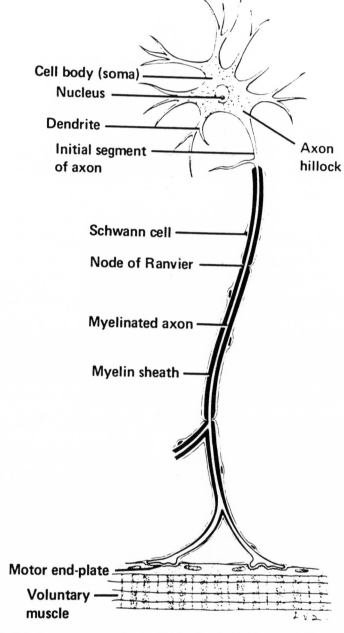

Cell body (soma)
Nucleus
Dendrite
Initial segment
of axon
Axon
hillock
Schwann cell
Node of Ranvier
Myelinated axon
Myelin sheath
Motor end-plate
Voluntary
muscle

Figure 2.0. Motor neuron with myelinated axon. (Reproduced, with permission, from Chusid, JG: Correlative Neuronanatomy and Functional Neurology, 16th ed. Lange, 1976.)

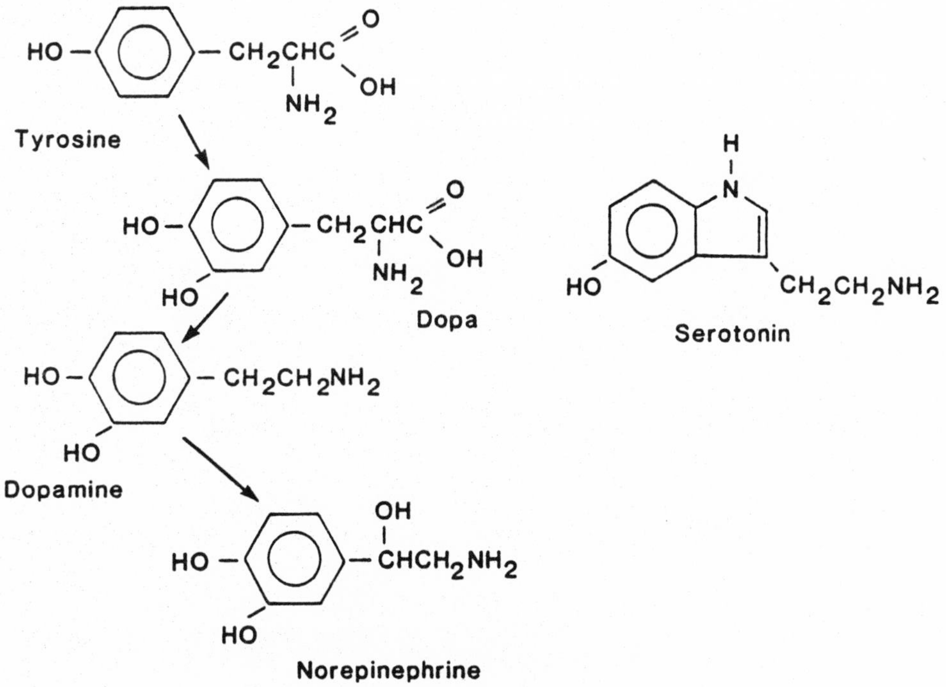

Figure 2.1. The biosynthesis of Norepinephrine from Tyrosine, and the neurotransmitter Seratonin.

ability of a neuron to transmit information to another is a function of its electrical transmission capability and its capacity to synthesize, store, and release a specific biochemical substance called a **neurotransmitter**. There are about some two dozen or more of these neurotransmitter substances, although, the function of only about six of them is understood at this time. These messengers are released from specific neurons after stimulation. Those chemicals considered to be neurotransmitters are: Dophamine (DA), Acetylcholine (Ach), Epinephrine (E), Norepinephrine (NE), Serotonin (5-HT), Gamma-aminobutyric acid (GABA), Glycine, Glutamate, and Histamine (Fig. 2.1).

The presynaptic part of a synapse contains a number of structures, in particular, mitochondria and synaptic vesicles. The vesicles contain some or all of the neurotransmitter substance. Once the neurotransmitter is released across the synaptic gap it interacts with the postsynaptic receptor (receptors are specialized structures that detect changes in the environment) (Fig. 2.3). The dynamics of this process is one of the most controversial in the field of neurobiology. Although our knowledge and understanding of this process is increasing, we are still far from definitive explanations.

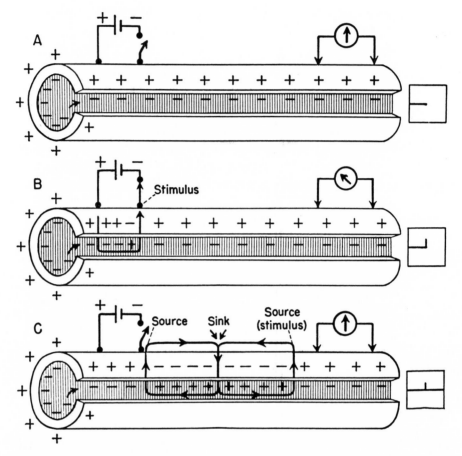

Figure 2.2. Diagram illustrating the initial changes following application of a stimulus to a nerve fiber. (A) The fiber is represented as a tube with a strip cut away so as to expose the interior. The stimulating electrodes, indicated by + and − , are at one end and the recording electrodes at the other. The electrical charges internal and external to the membrane are also indicated. (B) When the switch is closed, a battery current flows from the positive electrode into the fiber and out through the membrane back to the negative electrode (cathode), bringing about the change in membrane conductance. Some of the stimulating current leaks down the nerve, instantaneously for all practical purposes, and is recorded as a small deflection (inset at right). This is the shock artifact and indicates the moment of stimulation. (C) The effect of current flow out through the membrane is to initiate the conduction of a nerve impulse. The impulse is represented as two dipoles, each consisting of current flow (not the stimulating current from the battery) within a region indicated by the reversal of electrical charges. The current flow out through the membrane in the leading dipole acts as a stimulus, just as did the artificial current from the battery. (Reproduced, with permission, from Gardner E., Fundamentals of Neurology, Sixth Edition, W.B. Saunders, 1975.)

Protein molecules make up an important part of the receptor cell membrane. Their structure is highly specific for certain transmitters and they are believed to bind the transmitter in a "lock-and-key" arrangement. Binding of the transmitter results in receptor conformation producing specific changes in the membranes permeability for sodium and potassium. Thus, this causes the propagation of what is referred to as the action potentional (Fig. 2.2). Further, receptor-transmitter binding initiates a complex chain of intracellular reactions within the postsynaptic effector cell. This action is probably mediated via adenylate cyclase and cyclic AMP, which stimulate the cell to carry out its specific function.

The relationship between a transmitter and a receptor is an equilibrium process where transmitter molecules are repeatedly dissociating from the receptor, freeing it to be restimulated. Within the cholinergic system, neurotransmitter action is terminated at the postsynaptic membrane by an enzyme called acetylcholinesterase. For the catechol and indoleamine termination of a transmitters action depends upon washout of the synaptic gap by microcirculatory perfusion, postsynaptic degradation, or reuptake of the transmitter in the presynaptic neuron, the latter is of most importance.

PERIPHERAL NERVOUS SYSTEM

The peripheral nervous system consists of: (1) spinal nerves, 31 pairs arising from the spinal cord, one of each pair for the right side and the other for the left side of the body and (2) cranial nerves, 12 pairs arising from the brain, one of each pair for the right side and the other for the left side of the body.

Peripheral afferent (sensory) fibers are involved with sensations such as touch, temperature, and pain. Efferent (motor) fibers on the other hand are involved with the control of specific body functions. These fibers are divided into two separate categories: (1) somatic fibers, control skeletal muscle functions and (2) autonomic fibers, which control the activities of the involuntary actions of smooth muscles (intestines), cardiac muscle, blood pressure, and glands of secretion.

Somatic nerve fibers leave the spinal cord at various points, depending on the location of the innervated skeletal muscle. The site at which the somatic fiber meets the skeletal muscle is called the neuromuscular junction (NMJ). The neurotransmitter substance secreted at the NMJ is acetylcholine.

Autonomic efferent fibers control the unconscious functioning of the smooth, cardiac muscle and exocrine glands. Efferent fibers are responsible for activities such as the maintenance of tone in the gastrointestinal tract, blood vessels, regulation of heart rate, and release of substances such as respiratory secretions. Autonomic fiber tracts are of two types (1) the first fiber is called the presynaptic fiber which originates inside the spinal cord and ends at a synapse somewhere in the periphery and (2) the second fiber is called the postsynaptic fiber and originates at the synapse and ends at the innervated tissue. Whenever, the synapses of a number of fibers are grouped together, they are referred to as a ganglion. In incidences where this grouping occurs, the presynaptic and postsynaptic fibers are referred to as preganglionic and postganglionic fibers, respectively. The site where the postganglionic fibers synapse with innervated tissue is referred to as the neuroeffector junction (NEJ).

The autonomic fibers are categorized by two methods. The first classification is based on the sites at which preganglionic fibers exit the CNS. Those nerves that leave from the lumbar and thoracic areas of the spinal cord are called the sympathetic branch. Those nerves that exit from the sacral area of the spinal cord and cranium are called the parasympathetic branch. The sympathetic branch responds during times of arousal or emotional disequilibrium to prepare the body to respond to emergencies. Thus, activation of the sympathetic branch has been commonly referred to as the "flight or fight" mechanism because it prepares the body for a high level of activity. Epinephrine, plays a key role in the stimulation of adrenergic receptors for vigorous activity. Epinephrine is also released during stressful periods from the adrenal glands. It is then transported via the body to increase adrenergic activity. The sympathetic division is synchronized to produce mass action of all the systems under its control (Fig. 2.3).

The parasympathetic branch, on the other hand, is dominant when the individual is relaxed and at rest. However, it is most active only during periods of low arousal or relaxation and has the function of maintaining vital functions such as breathing and certain digestive processes.

The second method of classification is based on the release of a specific neurotransmitter substance at the NEJ by the nerve fibers. Nerves that release acetylcholine (ACH) are called cholinergic and those that release norepinephrine (NE) are called adrenergic. Generally, the term sympathetic is interchangeable with adrenergic while the term parasympathetic is interchangeable with cholinergic. Today, cholinergic and

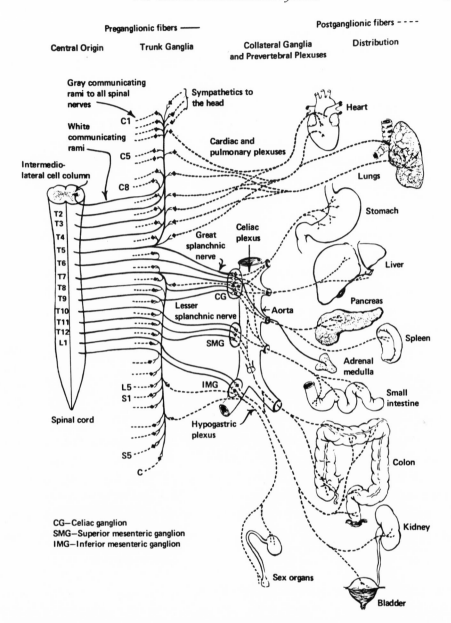

Figure 2.3. Sympathetic division of the autonomic nervous system (Reproduced, with permission, from Chusid, J.G., Correlative Neuroanatomy and Functional Neurology, 16th Edition, Lange Medical Publications, 1976.)

adrenergic are the terms preferred when discussing the effects of drugs on the ANS because they designate the specific neurotransmitter substance effected by the drug.

CHOLINERGIC RECEPTORS

There are three different types of peripheral cholinergic receptors.

1. Muscarinic receptors on effector cells innervated by postganglionic cholinergic fibers (all parasympathetic and some sympathetic postganglionic fibers). Muscarine is an alkaloid which, when isolated from certain poisonous mushrooms, mimics the effects of acetylcholine at these sites.

2. Ganglionic nicotinic receptors on ganglion cells innervated by preganglionic cholinergic fibers. Nicotine mimics the effects of ACH at this site and the action of both nicotine and ACH are blocked by hexamethonium which does not interfere with the muscarinic action of ACH.

3. Neuromuscular nicotinic receptors located on the motor endplates of striated muscles. Nicotine mimics the effects of ACH here and the action of both nicotine and ACH are blocked by D-tubocurarine but not by hexamethonium or atropine.

ADRENERGIC RECEPTORS

Receptors sites on cells innervated by postganglionic adrenergic fibers have varying pharmacological characteristics. These receptors are divided into two groups.

1. Alpha receptors, activated by norepinephrine, phenylephrine, and epinephrine. Specific drugs block the effects of agonists (a drug producing some response) on these receptors.

2. Beta receptors, activated by isoproterenol, epinephrine, and norepinephrine. Specific drugs block effects of agonists on beta receptors without changing their effects on alpha receptors. Beta receptors have been separated into Beta 1 and Beta 2 receptors based on relative selectivity of agonists and antagonists (Blocker).

THE CENTRAL NERVOUS SYSTEM

The CNS consists of the brain and the spinal cord. The spinal cord is a collection of nerve fibers (afferent and efferent) protected by the spine. In all vertebrate animals, the spinal cord carries out associational and motor functions. The brain occupies the cranium and has developed as a result of encephalization. The brain cavity is commonly of 1200 to 1500 ml capacity. There are many openings or foramina in the base of the skull for nerves and blood vessels. Through the foramen magnum, the medulla oblongata of the brain is continuous with the spinal cord.

The brain and the spinal cord are covered and protected by three layers of nonnervous tissue referred to as the **meninges**. The brain controls body functions and interacts with the external environment. The brain is composed of several distinct areas some of which function independently (structure) and others function more in an integrated (systems) fashion.

The primary structures of the brain are: (1) cerebral cortex, (2) thalamus, (3) hypothalamus, (4) medulla, and (5) pons. The primary systems of the brain include the limbic system, extrapyramidal system, and the reticular activating system. Some of these subcortical structures and systems are theorized to be implicated in the production of certain psychiatric disturbances, or to be effected by various psychotropic substances (Fig. 2.4).

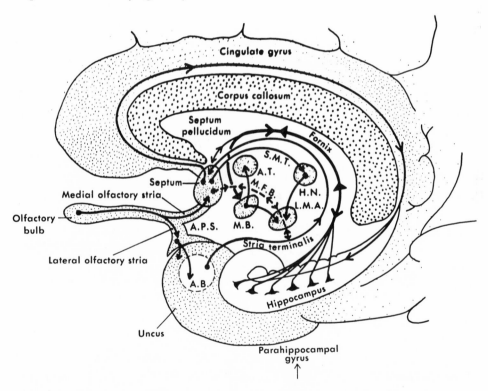

Figure 2.4. Schematic representation of some of the connections of the limbic system. Arrows indicate direction of conduction, and some structures carry fibers conducting in different directions. S.M.T., stria medullaris thalami; H.N., habenular nucleus; A.T., anterior thalamic nucleus (its projection to the cingulate cortex is omitted); M.F.B., medial forebrain bundle; L.M.A., limbic midbrain area; M.B., mamillary body; A.P.S., anterior perforated substance; A.B., amygdaloid body. (Reproduced, with permission, from Gardner, E., Fundamentals of Neurology, Sixth Edition, W.B. Saunders, 1975.)

Covering both hemispheres is a thin layer of cells referred to as the cerebral cortex. The cortex is involved with our ability to think, learn, remember, and is responsible for the highest level of integration for body functions. The cortex is also responsible for primary control of skeletal muscles and the interpretation of sensations. The cerebral cortex is divided into four lobes, each with a specific function.

1. Frontal Lobe—Involved in abstract thought and selective emotional responding.

2. Occipital Lobe—Concerned with vision.

3. Temporal Lobe—Interpretation of auditory stimulation.

4. Parietal Lobe—Interpretation of body sensation, e.g., pain, temperature, and orientation to time and space (Fig. 2.5 and 2.6).

The cortex is most sensitive to the action of many drugs. Depressants such as the barbiturates affect this area causing sedation, slurred speech, and ataxia. Stimulants on the other hand such as cocaine and amphetamines have an arousal affect on cortical function.

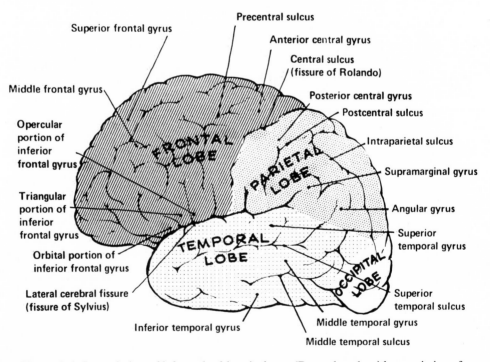

Figure 2.5. Lateral view of left cerebral hemisphere. (Reproduced, with permission, from Chusid, J.G., Correlative Neuroanatomy and Functional Neurology, 16th Edition, Lange Medical Publications, 1976.)

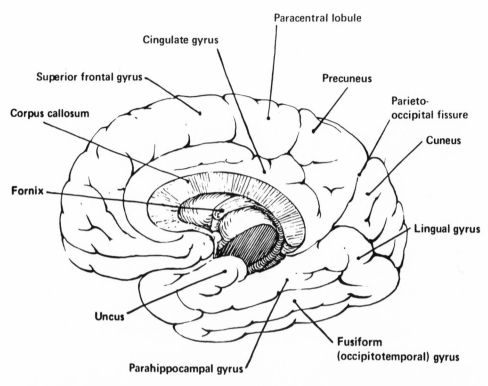

Figure 2.6. Medial view of right cerebral hemisphere. (Reproduced, with permission, from Chusid, J.G., Correlative Neuroanatomy and Functional Neurology, 16th Edition, Lange Medical Publications, 1976.)

Located subcortically are a group of structures involved in many specialized functions. Among these are the thalamus and hypothalamus which are located in an area of the brain referred to as the midbrain. The thalamus is often referred to as a relay station for purposes of information passing between the cortex and other brain areas. The epithalamus is involved with olfactory sensations and the penial gland, which is concerned with biochemical responses to illumination and hormonal control of sexual development. The subthalamus is concerned with some extrapyramidal system functions. Many drugs are known to affect the function of these structures. The opioid analgesics, for example, are one class of drugs which appear to produce their activity by blocking the transmission of pain impulses between the sensory cortex (parietal lobe) and the thalamus.

The hypothalamus serves as the output system for those emotions generated via the limbic system (emotional brain). The hypothalamus regulates functions of the endocrine gland by producing releasing factors that release hormones from the pituitary gland, thereby maintaining various homeostatic processes such as body temperature, blood pressure, and internal and external fluid volume.

There are certain drugs which depress the normal functions of the hypothalamus causing impairment of visceral functioning. Such drugs include the antipsychotics, barbiturates, and opioid analgesics. The medulla as indicated above is an extension of the spinal cord. The medulla plays a chief role in the control of autonomic functions. It is principally responsible for regulation of breathing, blood vessel tone, heart rate, and gastrointestinal tone. The medulla also contains the chemoreceptor trigger zone (CTZ) which elicits vomiting when stimulated by various chemicals.

The pons, just above the medulla, also serve an important regulatory function. The pons are involved in sleep patterns, especially slow-wave type, or nondream sleep.

The brain stem structures are least sensitive to the effects of drugs. However, under circumstances of overdose, drugs such as alcohol and barbiturates, which depress the CNS, can depress brain stem function. Thus, death may result from either respiratory depression or cardiovascular collapse.

Collectively, those structures previously mentioned above function interdependently to control specialized activities and are referred to as brain systems. The first system we will consider is the limbic system. Swonger and Constantine (1976) consider the limbic system the seat of emotions. A lesion or physiological dysfunction in the limbic system produces a wide range of abnormal psychological or behavioral phenomena. The limbic system is also called the rhinencephalon because of its relationship with olfaction.

Structures of the limbic system include: (1) amygdaloid complex, (2) hippocampus, (3) septal area, (4) limbic midbrain, and (5) other sites such as the hypothalamus, anterior thalamus, mamillary bodies, and frontal cortex. Primarily through the ANS, these structures form a system having the ability to originate and display emotions (Akert and Hummel, 1968). The amygdaloid complex is involved with the sense of smell, fear, aggressiveness, learning, and discrimination. The hippocampus is involved in both short-term and long-term memory (Swonger and Constantine, 1976).

The septal area is often referred to as the "pleasure area of the brain" because its stimulation is very rewarding to both animals and humans.

Also, the septal area controls some emotional behavior such as aggressiveness and the "startled" response.

The limbic midbrain area is involved with short-term memory and the ability to respond emotionally to particular stimuli. The limbic structures are interconnected by fiber tracts such as the medial forebrain bundle (MFB).

The MFB perhaps is the major pathway associated with pleasure. In its pathway, it uses the neurotransmitter NE. Other neurotransmitters involved with the limbic system include: (1) DA, (2) ACH, and (3) 5-HT. Currently, the role of these neurotransmitters is not fully understood. However, studies have indicated that decreased levels of both NE and serotonin have been associated with endogenous depression (Maas, 1975). An increased sensitivity of DA receptors or excessive synthesis or release of DA is associated with schizophrenia (Snyder, 1977). Perhaps, the relative balance of the neurotransmitters throughout the limbic system account for our normal emotional functioning.

The extrapyramidal system of the brain deals with basic, unskilled motor movements, as contrasted with the pyramidal (or coxtecospinal) system, which controls skilled (e.g., related to speech and fingers and hand) motor movements.

The development and widespread use of neuroleptics has intensified scientific interest in the extrapyramidal nervous system. It has been observed that: (1) neuroleptics reduce the amount of the brain chemical DA in the extrapyramidal regions of the brain called the substantia nigra, (2) low Parkinson's disease is highly associated with low DA levels, and (3) large doses of neuroleptics given to psychotic patients can induce signs of Parkinsonism. Current investigative research efforts have been centered on trying to determine what the role of the extrapyramidal system and DA is in maintaining mental stability.

The extrapyramidal systems primary structure includes the corpus striatum, substantia nigra, red nucleus, vestibular system, and the cerebellum. In addition, the brain stem reticular formation is involved in the flow of impulses from the extrapyramidal system into the spinal cord.

Finally, there are two other components of the extrapyramidal system, they are the vestibular system and the cerebellum. The vestibular system (inner ear) is associated with effects on posture and reflexes associated with balance. Receptors in this system can detect position of the head, acceleration, and the pull of gravity.

The cerebellum is involved with the control of muscle tone and in servomechanistic activities requiring hand-eye coordination. In other words, the cerebellum receives input from the motor cortex as well as from other extrapyramidal areas and makes whatever changes are necessary so that the intended function is performed.

Another of the brain's systems, called the reticular activating system (RAS), can also be altered by substance abuse. The RAS is a part of a larger system, the reticular formation (RF), a diffuse collection of nuclei found in both the medulla and midthalamus. The RAS is responsible for maintaining an alert conscious state. A lesion or chemical dysfunction in this area produces a decline in our level of alertness causing lethargy, stupor, and/or coma.

Two major syndromes associated with dysfunction of RAS are: (1) narcolepsy and (2) hyperkinesis. Narcolepsy is characterized by an inability to stay awake caused by a decreased ability of RAS to stimulate the cortex. Hyperkinesis, often seen in children is characterized by a short attention span, hyperactivity, and an inability to concentrate.

Finally, the RAS is involved in the control of the sleep-wake cycle. Until recently, it was believed that sleeping was a passive process made possible by a lack of cortical stimulation by the RAS. However, it is now known that sleep can be induced by stimulation of certain brain areas. Also, it is known that destruction of these areas produces insomnia. Therefore, the sleep-wake cycle should be more correctly considered as an active process controlled by specific brain areas.

Many of the psychoactive drugs that will be discussed in this text have an effect on the brain's peripheral and autonomic nervous systems. Additionally, because of their action, it should be understood that these drugs produce certain effects on the body as well.

The psychoactive drugs will be discussed according to the following classification: (1) sedative-hypnotics, (2) narcotic-analgesics (opiates), (3) stimulants, (4) hallucinogens, and (5) psychiatric drugs (neuroleptics and anxiolytics).

The sedative-hypnotics (alcohol, barbiturates, narcotics) are generalized central nervous system depressants. At low doses, they promote relaxation, and at higher doses, they induce sleep and stupor. At still higher doses, they produce coma and paralysis of the lower brain stem, causing death due to respiratory arrest.

Narcotics act primarily upon the central and parasympathetic nervous system, with powerful effects on pain perception, respiration, and smooth muscle response. It is not precisely known at this time how the opiates act on the brain. However, gross electroencephalograph (EEG) changes have been found which resemble those produced by the barbiturates. Also, the EEG patterns shift from that which is characteristic of alertness to that of drowsiness, then to that of sleep. The opiates, like the sedative-hypnotics, suppress REM (rapid eye movement) sleep.

Stimulants are a class of drugs that increase arousal and alertness by speeding up all of the brain and nervous system processes. At high doses, this classification of drugs causes anxiety, irritability, paranoid feelings, delirium, hallucinations, convulsive seizures, and toxic psychosis.

The hallucinogens produce powerful peripheral and central nervous system alterations. They are capable of dramatically altering parasympathetic and sympathetic activity as well as the activity of the reticular activating system (responsible for alertness of higher brain centers).

The exact structures in which the antipsychotic drugs exert their influence are not known. However, the effects of the antipsychotics probably occur either within the limbic system, where it is known that excitation of the hippocampus and the inhibition of the amygdala produce calmness and tranquility or at the hypothalamic level where the blocking of adrenergic transmission prevents sympathetic effects.

Inhalants are a specific class of substances that produce a wide range of effects. The acute effects of the inhalants range from mild inebriation that resembles alcohol intoxication to chemical psychosis with hallucinations, delusions, and gross behavior disturbances. Depending upon the particular inhalant, the chronic effects include neurologic abnormalities, liver and/or renal damage, vasodilation, hypotension, cancer pulmonary alveolitis, and death.

MODE OF ACTION OF THE PSYCHOTROPIC DRUGS; NEUROLEPTICS AND ANXIOLYTICS

The chemical substances thought to mediate the process of snyaptic transmission in the CNS are called neurotransmitters. Psychotropic drugs often exert their effects by altering the activity of neurotransmitters. In recent years, attention has been focused on the neurotransmitters known as the catecholamines (norepinephrine and dopamine) and the indolalkylamine, serotonin. Schizophrenia and effective disorders have been postulated to relate to the abnormal functioning of neural pathways involving these neurotransmitters.

Dopamine has been implicated in the etiology of schizophrenic symptoms. Currently, three major dopamine systems have been identified in the CNS: (1) the nigrostriatal pathway, (2) the mesolimbic pathway, and (3) the tubero-infundibular pathway. Some researchers have also identified a mesocortical dopamine system (Fig. 2.7).

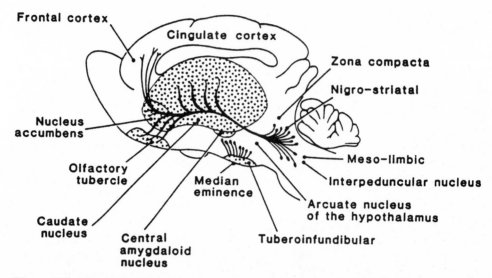

Figure 2.7. Schematic diagram indicating the distribution of the main central neuronal pathways containing dopamine. The stripped regions indicate the major nerve terminal areas. (Modified after U. Ungerstedt, Acta. Physiol. Scand. (1971) Suppl. 367.)

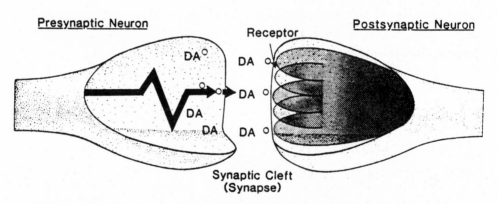

Figure 2.8. Diagrammatic representation of the normal process of release of dopamine. (Modified from Merrell Dow Pharmaceuticals.)

Within the dopaminergic system, dopamine is synthesized and stored in the presynaptic neuron. Upon sufficient excitation of this neuron, dopamine is released from the dendrites into the synaptic cleft. It diffuses across the cleft and attaches reversibly to the postsynaptic neuron. The transmitter attaches to sites on the postsynaptic neuron known as receptors. The neurotransmitter receptor complex initiates a chain of events which alternately results in the stimulation of the postsynaptic neuron (Fig. 2.8).

It is currently believed that many of the symptoms and signs of schizophrenia are related to the functional overactivity of a dopamine system in the mesolimbic and/or mesocortical areas. Symptoms such as loose associations, flat affect, hallucinations, and delusions respond significantly to antipsychotics such as Thorazine® and Haldol® which block dopamine at the postsynaptic receptor. The overall clinical efficacy of the antipsychotic (dopamine blocking) agents in schizophrenia has been documented in numerous double-blind studies. However, it must be pointed out that the interaction of several neurotransmitter systems has been observed. At present, the interaction of dopamine, norepinephrine, and other neurotransmitters has not been fully explained. It may be that the antipsychotic agents are thought to act predominantly on dopamine receptors, but their actions cannot be fully explained because of uncertainties in their effects on other neurotransmitters and their interactions. With adequate doses of antipsychotic drugs, patients may begin to show a reduction in psychotic signs and symptoms 48 hours after the administering of the initial doses. Full clinical recovery often takes several weeks or more.

The dopamine-blocking activity of the antipsychotics produces a number of side effects, often referred to as extrapyramidal symptoms. They include the following:

1. **Parkinson-Like Syndrome**—Including muscle tremor, drooling, muscle rigidity, slowed movements, shuffling gait, and postural abnormalities. These symptoms tend to occur more often in young adults, children, and women.

2. **Akathisia**—A compelling tendency toward constant movement, especially involving the lower extremities. These symptoms occur more often in elderly patients and women.

3. **Dyskinesia**—Facial, neck, back, or tongue spasms, difficulty in speaking, swallowing, and occulogyric crises. These symptoms may be accompanied by profuse sweating, pallor, and fever. These symptoms occur most often in children and men.

4. **Tardive Dyskinesia**—Stereotyped involuntary movements of tongue, lips, cheeks, and extremities.

Many of the extrapyramidal side effects of the neuroleptics can be blocked by the concurrent administration of medications such as Cogentin® or Blenadryl®. A discussion of their mechanism of action exceeds the intent of this chapter.

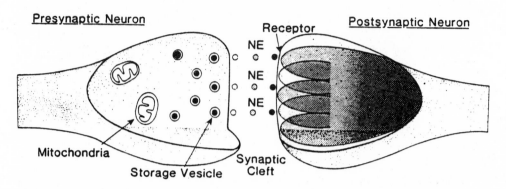

Figure 2.9. A schematic drawing showing the fate of Norepinephrine at the moment of release of the stored neurotransmitter is called Exocytosis. (NE = Norepinephrine; MAO = Monoamine Oxidase) (Courtesy of Merrell Dow Pharmaceuticals.)

The following is a list of some of the most commonly used neuroleptics: Thorazine®, Mellaril®, Trilafon®, Stelazine®, Navane®, Prolixin®, and Haldol®.

A number of classes of drugs—tricyclics, monoamine oxidase inhibitors, tetracyclics—have been shown to be effective in the treatment of depression. When used appropriately, they can facilitate an elevation of mood, a perceived increase in energy and motivation, increased appetite and libido, and improved sleep patterns. Unlike the neuroleptics, these medications often require several weeks before significant improvement occurs. Similar to the antipsychotic drugs, their actions are thought to be consequent to their ability to alter the activity of certain CNS neurotransmitters. It has been postulated that the signs and symptoms of depression are casually related to the activity of norepinephrine and serotonin at various areas of the brain. The antidepressants are thought to work by increasing the activity of the norepinephrine and/or serotonin at the postsynaptic receptor (Fig. 2.9).

Depression is thought to be relieved by increasing the amount of norepinephrine or serotonin which acts with the postsynaptic receptors. The tricyclic and tetracyclic antidepressants increase the amount of neurotransmitters available by blocking its reuptake into the presynaptic neuron. Reuptake into the presynaptic neuron results in the inactivity of the neurotransmitters (Fig. 2.10). Monamine oxidase inhibitors increase the amount of the available neurotransmitter by inhibiting inactivation by enzymes called monoamine oxidase (Figs. 2.11 and 2.12). The reader should realize that although these medications are capable of relieving depression, they are not considered stimulants because they do not possess the overwhelming CNS stimulation ascribed to that group of agents.

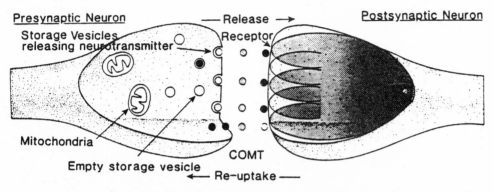

Figure 2.10. Diagrammatic representation of the normal process of release, re-uptake, and enzymatic metabolism of the neurotransmitter. (Courtesy of Merrell Dow Pharmaceuticals.)

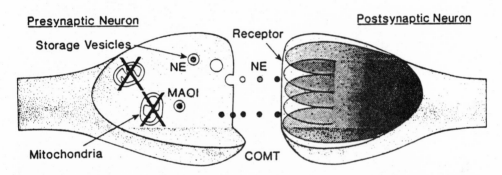

Figure 2.11. Diagrammatic representation of the mechanism of action of the Monoamine Oxidase Inhibitor. Norepinephrine is illustrated with a similar process being thought to occur with Serotonin (5HT) (NE = Norepinephrine; COMT = Catechol-o-methyl Transferase) (Courtesy of Merrell Dow Pharmaceuticals.)

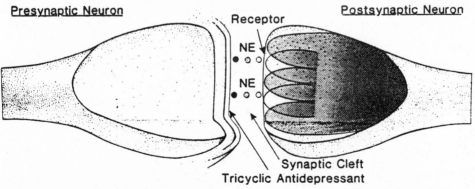

Figure 2.12. Diagrammatic representation of the mechanism of action of the Tricyclic Antidepressants. The Tricyclic Antidepressant blocks the presynaptic nerve terminal and thus the concentration is increased at the receptor site and the effects is potentiated. (NE = Norepinephrine) (Courtesy of Merrell Dow Pharmaceuticals.)

The tricyclic (e.g., Elavil®, Tofranil®, Asendin®), and Tetracyclic (e.g., Ludiomil®) antidepressants produce a number of problems or side effects. These include dry mouth, blurred vision, and effects on the cardiovascular system. They may also have potentially serious drug-drug interactions with other medications, such as those used to treat high blood pressure. The toxicity associated with these agents provides a convenient means to commit suicide for a population that is at high risk for suicide. For these reasons, tricyclics should be used cautiously and with close supervision.

A number of medications have been used in the treatment of anxiety. Meprobamate® was the first drug used in treating anxiety in patients in the late 1950's. More recently, the benzodiazepines (Librium®, Valium®, Ativan®, etc.) have become the most popular antianxiety agents. Due to the fact that anxiety is an ill-defined entity, it is difficult to develop an acceptable model or mechanism of action. Most antianxiety agents have a variety of clinical effects including sedation, muscle relaxation, anticonvulsant activity, and diminution of cognitive distress. Antianxiety agents also have a significant tendency for psychological and physiological habituation.

The benzodiazepines have a number of effects on several CNS neurotransmitters including a decrease in the turnover of norepinephrine and serotonin. They also alter the activity of other CNS neurotransmitters such as acetylcholine, glycine, and gamma-aminobutyric acid (GABA). GABA is generally accepted as being an inhibitory neurotransmitter in the brain and spinal cord. Some researchers postulate that much of the antianxiety action is secondary to an augmentation of GABA activity.

The antianxiety agents are the most frequently prescribed psychotropic medications. This is due, in part, to their almost immediate effect (within one hour) and their minimal side effects. These drugs are extremely safe. Taken alone, it is virtually impossible to die from their ingestion. This often results in their use to provide symptomatic relief without sufficient attention paid to the source of the anxiety. Due to their potential for abuse and addiction, antianxiety drugs are best used for brief periods and only when absolutely necessary.

REFERENCES

Akert, K., and Hummel, P. *The Limbic System Anatomy and Physiology*, Nutley, NM: Roche Laboratories, 1968.

Maas, J.W. Biogenic Amines and Depression, *Archives of General Psychiatry*, 32:1357-1361, 1975.

Snyder, S.H. Biochemical Factor in Schizophrenia, *Hospital Practice*, 12:133-140, 1977.

Swonger, A.K., and Constantine, L.L. *Drugs and Therapy*, Boston: Little, Brown, 1976.

Chapter 3

ALCOHOL

ALCOHOL IS a sedative-hypnotic drug, ether-like in origin, with the following chemical structure C_2H_5OH. There are many types of alcohol. First, methyl alcohol, commonly known as wood alcohol, is made by heating wood in the absence of air until it breaks down and then by collecting the vapors formed. Methyl alcohol is extremely toxic. As little as one ounce can produce irreversible blindness or death. Each year many accidents are attributed to mistaking methyl alcohol for its less harmful relative, ethyl alcohol. Second, ethyl alcohol is the intoxicating ingredient found in beverages such as beer, wine, brandy, whiskey, and vodka. Ethyl alcohol is the most commonly used and abused drug in the United States. It has been estimated that more than two-thirds of the adult American population drink alcoholic beverages at least occasionally. Although the majority of these individuals do so responsibly.

Ethyl alcohol is quite toxic. One pint of pure alcohol, rapidly ingested can kill most individuals. Even the strongest alcoholic beverages are no more than 90 proof (45% ethyl alcohol). The proof of any alcoholic beverage is merely twice the percentage of the alcohol by volume.

Ethyl alcohol is used in large amounts as an industrial solvent and as a starting material for other chemical products. Also, it is used as a preservative, and thus is found in tinctures and elixirs. Alcohol is used to cleanse, disinfect, harden the skin, and reduce sweating. Seventy-five percent alcohol is an effective bactericide. Although its use on open wounds is not recommended, because it will dehydrate the damaged tissue and make the injury worse. In addition, alcohol cools the skin by evaporation, thus, it is commonly used to reduce fever. Alcohol may be injected in or near nerve tissue to treat severe pain (local anesthetic). In

41

the elderly alcohol may facilitate appetite and digestion. Finally, physicians often prescribe alcohol in small doses for their geriatric patients as a sedative or tranquilizer.

ALCOHOLISM THE DISEASE

THE VALLEY OF TEARS

Alcoholism is a disease producing specific physical and psychological manifestations often referred to as chemical dependency. However, the concept of alcoholism as a disease has not yet been entirely accepted by the public at large. This is understandable since, while people may give recognition to the idea that alcoholism is an illness, many are inclined to feel that, at least, it is self-imposed. There is tremendous ignorance and emotional feelings associated with the disease of chemical dependency.

Today, there is no disease in America which is more capable of producing emotional upheaval in the nuclear or immediate family than alcoholism. Compared to the ingestion of other drugs, alcohol can be measured quite easily in the early user. However, the user soon begins to develop a dependency on the drug. This dependency and its associated euphoria, lead the alcoholic to more frequent and continued use of the drug. At a given point during the development of the addiction, the alcoholic begins to seek out the drug to achieve the euphoria. At this point, the abuser moves into what the author refers to as the **Valley of Tears** (A dimension of despair, loss of personal dignity, fear, and loneliness through which every chemically dependent person must pass on their journey to addiction) from which he cannot return without intervention. After entering the valley of tears, the user can never return to social drinking. The euphoria gives way to dysphoria, which leads to more frequent ingestion of the drug in a futile attempt to restore euphoria. As the addiction progresses, the dysphoric stage becomes the dominate stage, and the euphoric stage is seldom achieved if at all. It is important for the reader to understand that alcoholism is a journey—a journey that takes time. So, you cannot become an alcoholic unless you abuse and conversely you cannot abuse unless you use and this takes time. Therefore, it is a journey to first use, then abuse, and for some move into the valley of tears and develop the disease of chemical dependency. For most individuals, it is difficult for them to see that alcoholism like any other type of addiction is a journey. In the case of alcohol, it is not related to volume, dose, or duration. Addictionologists have established that five out of seven people who use drugs abuse them (Talbott, 1982). Regarding addiction one out of the five who abuses the drug will develop the disease of chemical dependency, but two out of the five will abuse more than the person who is diseased. Thus, addiction is a most unique disease having a number of factors contributing to its onset. As the author views it, three factors are responsible for drug addiction. The first factor is simply the **use** of one of the mood-altering drugs. Second, is an individual's **vulnerability** to develop the disease because of physical (e.g., anatomical, biochemical), genetic, and/or psychological factors. Finally, **drug abuse** is the use of a drug for other than medicinal purposes which results in the impaired physical, mental, emotional, or social well-being of the user.

One way to illustrate this relationship between use, abuse, and vulnerability is through the use of moving, at times overlapping circles (Fig. 3.0). The three circles here represent the factors I have discussed above. The area where all three circles overlap may be thought of as the valley of tears dimension mentioned above.

As one views the illustration, each circle should be thought of as moving away from and/or toward the other depending on the importance of the three groups of variables. These circles are always in a constant and fluid motion. Each circle varies symbolically in size and with time. Whenever, the symbolic circle of vulnerability shifts away from the other circles (i.e., to the right so there is no overlap), there will be no addiction. The same is obtained if the user circle moves to the left. In this scheme, drug use obviously plays a major contributory role in the development of the disease of chemical dependency, because you can't abuse unless you use. A person can withstand the effects of high abuse if the individual's use and vulnerability are quite low.

As a consequence of the configuration of the circles, the individual now is set for the disease. The person is no longer making a cognitive choice to abuse the drug because of peer pressure or a bad marriage, he now needs the drug and will engage in antisocial and/or criminal behavior to obtain it. The reader must keep in mind that the addiction which the individual experiences is not for the drug per se but for the feelings that the drug produces for him. Thus, this is a different anatomical, biochemical, bioelectrical relationship from the usage, abusive, cognitive, controlled drug-taking behavior seen above. Chemical dependency, thus, tells us that the message to take the drug is compulsive, noncognitive, and noncontrolled behavior.

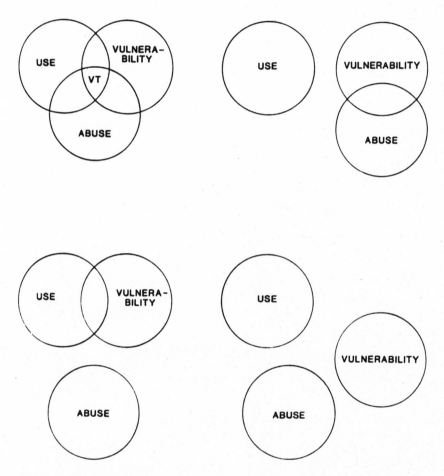

Figure 3.0. Diagram illustrating the use, abuse, and vulnerability concept.

Several explanations have been presented to understand this compulsive, noncognitive, and noncontrolled behavior — one is biochemical. Recently, it has been pointed out in the literature that the human body produces chemicals for its own natural high. Several investigators began searching for these chemicals and soon discovered not one but several. Each was a short peptide chain, composed of amino acid units. Those with 5 amino acid units are called enkaphalins. Those with 30 amino acid units are endorphins. They are both seen to be derived from the pituitary peptide called beta-lipotropin (Snyder, Snyder, 1977). Deep sensory nerves are stimulated by vigorous exercise which causes a release of the endorphins. Long-distance runners, for example, experience many of the symptoms that opiate users do. They get euphoric highs both during and after a hard workout. They also experience withdrawal when they refrain from vigorous exercise for prolonged periods of time. In those individuals whose brains lack these essential chemicals it decreases their ability to experience the feel good signal. Therefore, they are more vulnerable to develop the disease called chemical dependency.

Chronic abuse of alcohol has a deleterious effect on many organ systems. This section will discuss only those syndromes related to the physiological and psychological effects of alcohol abuse.

GASTROINTESTINAL SYSTEM

Alcohol has two basic effects on the body; (1) an irritant and (2) a sedative. When alcohol is consumed, it first travels through the esophagus to the stomach. While in the stomach, it may cause irritation and later inflammation of the stomach walls. This produces a condition called gastritis. Whenever gastritis is exacerbated, a severely irritated area develops on the walls of the stomach which is called an ulcer. Ulcers that form in the stomach are referred to as gastric ulcers and those in the first section of the intestine are duodenal ulcers.

What are the complications of ulcers when related to the consumption of alcohol? There are three major complications: (1) Bleeding of the inflamed tissue. If there is a large blood vessel in the area that the ulcer develops, a major massive hemorrhage may occur. (2) Perforation. If the ulcer is deep enough, it will perforate the wall of the stomach or intestines. Should this occur, the contents of the stomach will empty into the abdominal cavity. This condition will require immediate surgical intervention. (3) Obstruction. The inflammation of the lining of the stomach causes the tissue to swell. Inflammation of the esophagus or the small opening to the stomach leading to the intestines will prevent the passage of food into the stomach with a subsequent regurgitation of food. Vomiting in any situation can be dangerous because the victim not only empties his/her stomach, but also, air from the lungs, causing the individual to take in a deep breath. Food that is not ejected may be pulled back into the lungs, resulting in a blockage of the airway. Death from choking can occur within four minutes. If the individual survives this occurrence, he/she may develop a condition called aspiration pneumonia.

Ninety-five percent of the alcohol that is ingested is rapidly absorbed into the bloodstream. Complete absorption is slowed down.

In the small intestines, chronic alcoholism may cause a condition known as malabsorption syndrome. This disorder prevents the absorption of nutrients such as vitamins (vitamin B group) which contributes to the malnutrition that is often seen in the chronic alcoholic. Also, there is an increase in the excretion of many of the important minerals. The essential minerals include zinc, magnesium, and other trace metals. Alcohol washes calcium from the bones. This is an important factor for the elderly to consider before drinking. Demineralization of bones, often referred to as Osteoporosis, is exacerbated by the use of alcohol (Taylor, 1982).

ALCOHOL AND THE PANCREAS

The pancreas is an important organ that is adversely affected by alcohol. The pancreas secretes very important digestive enzymes which help us to digest proteins and fats in the small intestines. When the alcohol reaches the pancreas, it irritates the cells, causing them to swell and block the excretion of the enzymes. As these chemicals begin to accumulate, they eventually digest the pancreatic tissue itself. This condition is known as acute hemorrhagic pancreatitis. It is an extremely painful disease which requires administration of large amounts of analgesics to relieve the pain. About one out of ten patients who develop this disease die during their first attack.

The pancreas also functions to produce a chemical called insulin. Insulin is necessary for regulation of carbohydrate metabolism. Whenever there is an inappropriate supply of insulin, we have a condition known as diabetes. Usually, diabetes is a hereditary disease in which the pancreas does not produce or release enough insulin. However, as a result of the chronic use and abuse of alcohol, secondary diabetes sometimes develops. If not treated properly by adequate control of diet and/or medication, serious consequences and even death may occur (Taylor, 1982).

ALCOHOL AND THE LIVER

The liver is an important organ that is seriously affected by the use of alcohol. If the liver is irritated by alcohol or any other chemical, cells of the liver begin to swell, causing several things to occur. First lymphatic vessels in the liver are blocked off. Second, liver cells become inflamed, thus preventing the filtration of old blood cells and toxic wastes through the liver. Waste products from these old blood cells accumulate in the blood. Additional symptoms can occur, (i.e., the whites of the eyes begin to turn yellow, urine turns orange, and the skin turns yellow). This condition is known as jaundice. The reader should also keep in mind that this condition can be the direct result of other medical conditions such as cancer. Remember, anything that inflames the liver can cause this condition. Inflammation of the liver is referred to as hepatitis or alcoholic hepatitis.

Another condition associated with chronic use of alcohol is cirrhosis or scarring of the liver. Whenever this occurs, the normal functioning of the liver diminishes and it becomes more difficult to maintain good health. Those normal functions that are interfered with are the following: (1) The ability to ward off infections is diminished because of the inappropriate amounts of globulin being produced; (2) Loss of prothrombin, a chemical needed for clotting of the blood. An individual abusing alcohol suddenly develops hemorrhagic gastritis or an ulcer and he/she has a decreased prothrombin production. This may result in a massive hemorrhage. Due to the loss of the alcoholics ability to produce prothrombin, one of the most commonly seen complications of alcoholics is a subdural hemorrhage; (3) The increase in fatty acids and cholesterol which constrict blood vessels of the heart, as well as blood vessels of the extremities causing varicose veins in the legs, rectum, and along the sides of the abdomen. Consequently, the circulation of blood back to the heart and liver is slowed. However, there can be other causes of this condition such as pregnancy; (4) The ability of the liver to detoxify various chemicals, drugs, and foods. As long as the liver is healthy, it can metabolize one ounce of alcohol per hour. However, if the liver is not functioning properly, its ability to detoxify alcohol or any other substance is severely decreased. The more damage that is done to the liver, the longer the substance will remain in the bloodstream. Consequently, we begin to see small amounts of alcohol and other drugs and toxic substances linger on for long periods of time (Taylor, 1982).

ALCOHOL AND THE KIDNEYS/SEX ORGANS

Another organ that is severely harmed by the effects of alcohol is the kidney. Alcohol irritates the kidneys and causes them to secrete large amounts of fluids. When the alcohol content of the bloodstream has reached its maximum, the brain triggers the release of an antidiuretic hormone which causes retention of fluids in the body which results in swelling of tissue. Alcohol also affects the prostate gland which is referred to as prostatitis. The prostate gland is one of the organs important in the sexual behavior of males. There are at least two important events which occur whenever alcohol irritates this organ. First, urination becomes more difficult because of the restriction of urine flow from the bladder. Second, there is an interference with the ability to have or maintain an erection. There is also difficulty in having an orgasm during sexual intercourse. The prolonged abuse of alcohol further produces testicular atrophy or shrinking of the testicles. The inability of a diseased liver to detoxify as well as remove the female hormone estrogen, interferes with a man's sexual ability and may increase his breast size. Young adults consuming alcohol on a regular basis should be made aware of these effects on their developing bodies (Taylor, 1982).

Women experience a higher incidence of menstrual irregularities resulting from prolonged use of alcohol. Sexual potency is also diminished by the effects of alcohol. Another issue of importance to women today is the relationship between alcohol and pregnancy. It has been found that under certain circumstances, alcohol consumed by an expectant mother can have harmful effects on the unborn child.

Fetal alcohol syndrome (FAS) is the name given by researchers in 1973 to a consistent pattern of physical, mental, and behavioral problems observed in infants born to women who consumed heavy amounts of alcohol during their pregnancy. The children severely affected by this syndrome display: (1) mental retardation, (2) heart defects, (3) cleft palate, (4) joint and limb anomalies, (5) small heads, (6) facial irregularities, and (7) failure to thrive.

The explanation for this is not unlike any other substance ingested by the pregnant woman. The alcohol travels across the placenta into the fetus's bloodstream in the same concentration as it does through the mother's. However, the developing fetus' liver is only about half as efficient at metabolizing alcohol as an adult liver. Thus, the alcohol remains in the fetus' system for a longer period of time.

Researchers do not agree fully on the level of drinking that will cause fetal alcohol syndrome. The syndrome has been linked to heavy consumption during pregnancy (six drinks per day). However, other investigators have indicated that only moderate drinking (one to four per day) may increase the chances of spontaneous abortion; lower birth weight, central nervous system damage, lowered intelligence quotient, and unusual physical development.

Since a high blood alcohol level during a critical time of fetal development is necessary to cause fetal alcohol syndrome, the average daily consumption of small amounts of alcohol may not be as important as very heavy drinking at critical periods.

Even more complicated is the fact that two different pregnant women who expose their unborn fetuses to the same amount of alcohol may have entirely different effects. This may be due to genetic influences, whether the alcohol was consumed all at once, or distributed over a period of time. In any event, it may be critical for some.

Since alcohol has dangerous side effects, it would be a serious misconception on the part of women to think that only alcoholic mothers place their fetuses at risk. It is now known that moderate amounts of alcohol during pregnancy may prevent the unborn child from developing in a normal fashion.

Above are only some of the damaging effects that are often seen in individuals who use and abuse alcohol for long periods of time. It may be of some consequence for the reader to also explore the psychological effects of alcohol on the brain.

Of all the drugs, alcohol represents the most serious health hazard to the public. It accounts for over 50 percent of first admissions to psychiatric facilities and is associated with more than half of all automobile accidents. Alcohol also increases the rate of suicide among its users.

The incidence of alcoholism in the United States is estimated to be around ten million people. Its impact is felt in every aspect of life such as family, employment, and friends. Moreover, some 31 percent of all arrests in this country are for public drunkenness.

The World Health Organization defines alcoholism as excessive drinking in which the person is dependent on alcohol to such an extent that he/she shows disturbances in his/her mental and physical health, interpersonal relationships, and social and economic functioning. Thus, alcoholism is not just an addiction, but compulsivity.

The consequences of chronic alcoholism are acute psychological and physiological reactions such as confusion, excitement, and delirium. All of these reactions are labeled acute or chronic brain disorders. One such condition of an acute form is pathological intoxication. This reaction occurs when the tolerance to alcohol is very low, sometimes due to such things as stress, exhaustion, and other conditions. Whenever persons with this low tolerance consume small amounts of alcohol, they become confused, disoriented, and occasionally violent. This state usually results in deep sleep with complete retrograde amnesia afterwards (Taylor, 1982).

ALCOHOL WITHDRAWAL

Physical dependence on alcohol is dramatically demonstrated by the emergence of a withdrawal syndrome upon decrease in the blood alcohol

concentration of the abuser. The length of time which drinking has occurred and the amount consistently consumed are often closely related
to the severity of the withdrawal symptoms (Mello and Mendelson,
1976).

The consequences of alcoholism are severe. Delirium tremens (DT's)
for instance is a term used to describe the most advanced progression of
the alcohol withdrawal syndrome. Mortality due to DT's is up to 15 percent. However, the rate of mortality can be lowered to about 1 percent
with early recognition of the syndrome, aggressive pharmacotherapy,
and improved therapy for the physical complications of alcohol withdrawal (Sellers and Kalant, 1976; Victor and Laureno, 1978).

The symptoms of DT's develop 60 to 80 hours after drinking has
stopped (Fig. 3.1). DT's can be a frightening experience for the alcoholic. In addition to very intense visceral and somatic symptoms, the alcoholic may experience paranoid delusion, terrifying hallucinations
(snakes, elephants, and small animals), extreme suggestibility, tremors
of the hands, tongue, lips and convulsive seizures. Physiological symptoms include perspiration, fever, rapid heart beat, and increased respiration.

Another serious symptom of alcoholism is acute alcoholic hallucino-
sis, with the main symptom being auditory hallucinations. The individual hears voices, usually making critical or sarcastic remarks about personal weaknesses. Panic often occurs and the individual may scream or
attempt suicide.

Finally, there is Korsakoff's syndrome, which is a serious form of organic brain disease. Alcoholics with this disease display signs of ataxia
and aphasia. They also show signs of both retrograde amnesia and an-
terograde amnesia. In the former, the alcoholic cannot remember past
events, and in the latter, he/she cannot retain recent events. Whenever
the alcoholic is asked to recall past events, he/she does not remember so
they invent a story to fill in memory gaps. Confabulation is the filling in
of these memory gaps with obviously false material. Korsakoff's Psychosis is a disorder primarily of behavior and thought processes.

Alcoholism is a horrible disease which is often fatal, and can only be
interrupted by proper recognition and proper treatment (Taylor, 1982).

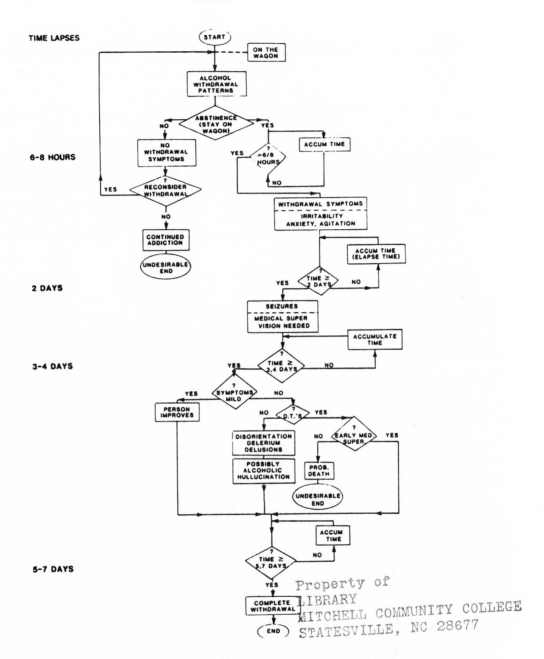

Figure 3.1. Flowchart of alcohol withdrawal patterns. In alcohol withdrawal, withdrawal patterns will begin as soon as the decision to remain abstinent is made. If abstinence is not chosen, no withdrawal patterns will be noted, unless withdrawal is reconsidered at a later time. If abstinence is not reconsidered, continued addiction will lead to no further withdrawal patterns and an undesirable termination. Once abstinence is chosen, the first withdrawal symptoms will appear in approximately six to eight hours. These symptoms ➡

52*Substance Abuse*

REFERENCES

Mello, N.K., and Mendelson, J.H. The Development of Alcohol Dependence: A Clinical Study, *McLean Hospital Journal*, 1:64-84, 1976.

Sellers, E.M., and Kalant, H. Alcohol Intoxication and Withdrawal, *New England Journal of Medicine*, 294(4):757-762, 1976.

Snyder, Solomon H. "The Brain's Own Opiates," *Chemical and Engineering News*, 26-35, November 28, 1977.

Snyder, Solomon H. "Opiate Receptors and Internal Opiates," *Scientific American*, 44-56, March, 1977.

Talbott, D.G. National Symposium on Psychiatry/*Chemical Dependence*, Atlanta, Georgia, October 26-29, 1982.

Taylor, P., Jr., *Psychoactive Drugs*, Burgess Publishing Company, 1982.

Vanthiel, D.E., and Lester, R. Alcoholism: Its Effects on Hypothalamic Pituitary Gonadal Function, *Gastroenterology*, 71:318-327, 1976.

include irritability, anxiety, and agitation. As time goes by, the symptoms of the first stage of withdrawal may reoccur before the next stage is reached, or the subject may go directly into the next stage. This cycle of reoccurring symptoms may continue for as long as two days before the second stage of symptoms appear. Seizures with medical supervision needed is the second stage of alcohol withdrawal symptoms. These may occur over a period of three to four days before the subject reaches the third stage of withdrawal. In the third critical stage of alcohol withdrawal, the subject may have mild symptoms which will lead to a general improvement and a complete withdrawal with a favorable end. If the symptoms are not mild, then the subject will continue to the D.T. stage. If the subject does not experience D.T.'s, then the next stage including disorientation, delirium, and delusions will lead directly to possible alcoholic hallucinations before complete withdrawal and a favorable termination. If the subject does experience D.T.'s, then early medical supervision should be obtained to bring the subject into complete withdrawal and a favorable termination. If early medical supervision is not obtained, then death will probably result in an undesirable end.

Chapter 4

CNS STIMULANTS

AMPHETAMINES (SPEED)

AMPHETAMINES were first synthesized by a California pharmacologist named George A. Alles in 1927. After discovering that amphetamines could possibly serve as a suitable substitute for ephedrine, and also be absorbed into the body by inhalation, Alles turned his patent over to Smith Kline and French Laboratories. There, a scientist discovered that a pronounced vasoconstrictive effect had been found with amphetamines and a recommendation was made that the drug be used in its vaporous state for relieving upper respiratory infections. Thus, Smith, Kline and French Laboratories introduced the first Benzedrine inhaler in 1932 (Griffenhagen, 1972). Later investigation led to the discovery that obese patients taking the drug lost their appetite which was helpful in weight loss. Dexedrine was introduced in 1945 because of its effectiveness to control weight gain and food consumption (Taylor, 1982).

Airmen, during World War II, relied on amphetamines for extra energy and alertness when flying long missions of considerable danger. Amphetamines were also used when the automatic controls failed to function properly in Astronaut Gordon Cooper's spaceship. Cooper was ordered to take an amphetamine capsule in order that his reflexes would increase when reentering the earth's atmosphere on manual controls.

Media accounts concerning the stimulating effects of Benzedrine led to its notoriety and abuses. The first known abuse occurred in 1936 at the University of Minnesota by students in a psychology class. In this class, students were conducting experiments with different drugs and tried Benzedrine themselves. These students found that Benzedrine helped them to stay awake in order to "cram" for exams. Later, the drug became very popular in many walks of life. Housewives, truck drivers, basketball players, and doctors began to take Benzedrine as a "pick-me-up" or as "pep" pills (Griffenhagen, 1972).

Misuse of these drugs brought about legal control in the United States. Benzedrine was placed on the prescription legend classification list, therefore, causing many individuals to seek other avenues of supply.

Amphetamines are a class of drugs that increase behavioral arousal and alertness, combat fatigue, sleepiness, and elevate mood. Amphetamines' ability to cause arousal and/or alertness is made possible because of the action amphetamines exert on the central and autonomic nervous systems. However, the action of these drugs is far more complex than their class implies. The brain is not a simple machine that can be simply stimulated by "uppers" and calmed or slowed by "downers." The fact of the matter is that there exists a misconception on the streets that one should treat an overdose with uppers and vice versa. The brain simply does not work in this fashion, nor do these drugs (Taylor, 1982).

Within the central nervous system, nerve tissue is stimulated by this class of drugs. The action of amphetamines causes a variety of complex chemicals to be released or inhibited at the sites in the brain where they function (Taylor, 1982). Depressants in the central nervous system have a corresponding effect, often at the same site as the stimulants, but also in other areas of the brain where the stimulants apparently have no effect.

In part, this may explain the wide range of effects seen in different individuals. Some amphetamines can make a person feel more alert, excited, talkative, and apprehensive, as well as produce an increase in blood pressure, euphoria, depression, convulsions, and toxic psychosis. The behavioral effects of the amphetamines are similar to those of cocaine, they differ in that amphetamines have a much longer duration of action than cocaine. Thus, there is a greater potential for adverse reaction and severe toxicity with the amphetamines than with cocaine (Bennett, Vourakis and Woolf, 1983).

Among the drugs considered in this class are amphetamine (Benzedrine), dextroamphetamine (Dexedrine), methamphetamine (Methedrine), cocaine, phenmetrazine (Preludin), methylphenidate (Ritalin), caffeine (coffee, tea, cola drinks, aspirin, over-the-counter antifatigue preparations), nicotine (cigarettes, cigars, snuff, smoking tobacco). Other stimulants include Bacarate, Cylert, Didrex, Lonamine, Pondimin, Pre-Sate, Sanorex, and Voranil.

Amphetamines produce three major effects upon the individual. First, amphetamines produce an awakening effect upon the individual.

Therapeutically, they are used in the treatment of narcolepsy and used to treat children diagnosed as being hyperactive. Second, the amphetamines are used for their appetite-suppressing ability. Amphetamines have been prescribed for obese persons in an effort to control their weight problems. However, the consequences in many cases have met with unfortunate results. Third, amphetamines induce a feeling of euphoria such that the individual believes that he can perform better on different tasks (Taylor, 1982).

Although amphetamines are not physically addicting, withdrawal symptoms experienced by "speed freaks" can be filled with misery and terror. Often the "speed freaks" inject Methedrine directly into their veins, feel euphoria for several days, then "crash" for several days, and begin the process all over again. Inevitably, paranoid and aggressive feelings begin to dominate a "speed freak's" personality. As a result of this chronic abuse of the amphetamines, a "toxic psychosis" emerges which is undistinguishable from the paranoid schizophrenic (Ellenwood, 1967). Homicidal or suicidal acts are also occasionally seen. There is evidence that permanent brain damage results from the abuse of this drug as well as impaired ability to concentrate, learn, and remember.

Recently, there have been many products containing the same ingredients as the stimulant drugs, but are produced by less well-known pharmaceutical companies. These drugs have become quite popular in many communities and are called "peashooters," "look-a-likes," or even "turkey drugs." These drugs have a remarkable physical resemblance to controlled prescription drugs (e.g. amphetamines) marketed for the same purpose. However, they contain caffeine, phenylpropanolamine and/or ephedrine which are central nervous system stimulants with decongestant, appetite suppressant, and stimulant properties. The use of these drugs in the short-term management of weight problems is controversial, but there is agreement that their adverse medical effects cause hypertension, cardiac arrhythmias, hemorrhagic stroke, irritability, paranoid psychosis, aggressiveness, confusion, hallucinations, seizures, and death (Taylor, 1982).

Abuse of the "peashooters" involves a number of factors. First, individuals purchase these drugs in bulk (1,000 to 12,000) thus saving as much as 75 percent of the across-the-counter price for the same quantity. Second, other individuals seek the amphetamine type "high" with these drugs rather than for their weight reducing effects. Third, people purchase these drugs with the expressed intent of selling them on the open market as amphetamines. Thus, the unsuspecting consumer may be "ripped-off." The fraudulent sale of these "peashooters," therefore, poses a serious health problem. The rationale for this is that individuals consuming several "peashooters" per dose might eventually buy some corresponding amphetamine, and while consuming the same number of tablets, increase the risk of a possible resultant overdose (Drug and Poison Information Center, University of Cincinnati, 1982).

COCAINE

The discovery and the eventual isolation of cocaine from the coca leaves is usually attributed to a Viennese by the name of Niemann, who isolated the compound in 1858. However, an early researcher by the name of Mariana who produced many different preparations of cocaine for therapeutic application, claimed that Gardeke was the first to discover the drug which he named "Erytroxyline" (Griffenhagen, 1972).

Cocaine has a powerful topical anesthetic action with a concomitant vasoconstrictive effect. Cocaine is used as an adjunct in surgery and in procedures involving highly vascular mucous membranes (e.g., nose and throat). According to Dr. George Gay, cocaine has two interrelated pharmacological actions: (1) it is a local anesthetic of high efficacy and relatively high toxicity, exerting its action by blocking nerve conduction at the cellular membrane, and (2) it is a powerful CNS stimulant of relatively short duration that manifests a relatively low margin of safety. Its action depends largely on site and route of administration, and is likewise markedly affected by individual variability, i.e., current emotional and physiological state of the individual, ambient climate, and general physical setting. The individual's ability to metabolize and excrete cocaine also affects the CNS.

Cocaine is extracted from the leaves of the coca bush (Erythroxylon). The coca leaf contains from .7 percent to 1.8 percent alkaloids of which the cocaine is about 30 to 75 percent of the total alkaloids in the leaf. The coca bush may be found in countries such as Ecuador, Bolivia, Columbia, and Peru (Taylor, 1982).

For almost 30 years after its discovery, cocaine was only viewed with curiosity by the medical community. It was not until 1884, when Sigmund Freud obtained a supply of the drug, that cocaine's potential for weaning morphine addicts was attempted. Freud and a colleague, Carl Koller, began a series of studies on the psychological effects of cocaine. Freud was to later write concerning his personal use of cocaine.

I discovered in myself, and in other observers who were capable of judging such things...that...even repeated doses of coca produce no compulsive desire to use the stimulant further; on the contrary, one feels a certain unmotivated aversion to the substance.

Shortly after the investigations had begun, Freud took a trip to visit his fiancee and Koller continued the research which later led to the discovery of cocaine's important anesthetic effects (Strachey, 1952).

Koller's discovery led to great interest among physicians in both private and hospital settings to experiment with cocaine. Lewis Lewin wrote about men of science using cocaine in this manner.

...I have seen among men of science frightful symptoms due to the craving for cocaine. Those who believe they can enter the temple of happiness through this gate of pleasure speedily pass through the gate of unhappiness into the night of the abyss. The pursuit of science is not enough to prevent folly. (Grassroots, 1972).

In the late nineteenth century, cocaine became a prime ingredient in an excessive number of patient medicines and "home remedies." Preparations such as Dr. Pemberton's French Wine of Coca, Ideal Tonic, and many others began to be seen on store shelves across the United States.

In 1902, a survey conducted by Crothers revealed that only about 3 to 8 percent of the total amount of cocaine sold throughout the entire nation went into the practice of medicine, dentistry, and veterinary medicine. Until the passage of the Pure Food and Drug Laws in 1906, the presence of cocaine in soft drinks (Coca Cola®) and drug store "soda fountain" preparations went unhampered.

In 1914, the Harrison Narcotic Act went into effect which classed cocaine with morphine and other narcotics. The drug's recreational uses were then driven underground resulting in an explosion of use in the decades to follow. Current users may wish a closer look at the effects of cocaine on the brain.

The use and abuse of cocaine has a deleterious effect on the brain itself. The brain is composed of billions of nerve cells which communicate continuously through a system of electrical and biochemical reactions. These chemicals in the brain are called neurotransmitter substances. Among the most well known are dopamine and endorphins which produce the feelings of well-being, happiness, and pleasure.

Cocaine effects the dopamine centers of the brain, causing alterations of the amounts of the chemical stored. Dopamine naturally increases our feelings of energy, power, and sexuality. However, the cocaine abuser falsely feels powerful, energetic, and sexual after injesting the drug. Therefore, cocaine may be said to short-circuit the natural pleasure centers of the brain. Thus, whenever cocaine activates these pleasure centers, it is activating the same centers which cause us to feel normal pleasures in response to love and accomplishment. As a result, cocaine damages the brain's physical ability to feel pleasure naturally, i.e., the brain becomes chemically less capable which causes emotions to become dull and memories weak. For those who suffer from severe addiction, it requires more of the drug to stop the pain the drug produced in the first place. Addiction, however, is not necessary to produce these feelings. Depletion of the brain's natural chemical balance by the use of cocaine will produce feelings of depression, withdrawal, and aggression with continued use. The reader should be mindful that recent evidence suggests that these effects may be permanent.

Recently, cocaine has been used in a process called "free basing." This is accomplished by dissolving street pure cocaine in certain solvents, adding other chemicals, and precipitating out purified cocaine which is then rolled into a cigarette and smoked (Taylor, 1982). Free basing is very dangerous because of the potential risk of fire and explosion. Also, there is considerable danger through smoking because it takes about six seconds to reach the brain. The faster it gets to the brain, the more intense the euphoria, the deeper and more severe the depression that follows. With such a depression, there is a tendency to hurry another high. Thus, developing an insidious cycle that encourages repeated, compulsive use and ultimate dependence, and increased danger of overdose. Early reports suggested that cocaine was a relatively benign drug and rarely if ever could it lead to overdose death. Cocaine overdose should always be considered as a life-threatening situation by clinicians. Overdose reactions may include simple anxiety, seizures, cardiac arrest, toxicity, and psychosis (Taylor, 1982).

Since cocaine is similar to a naturally occurring catecholamine, it tends to augment their effects. As the dosage level is increased, the user may begin to show signs of taking on an "armed posture against the outside world." The initial effect of excitement may be replaced by restlessness, irritability, and apprehension, along with stereotyped movements such as picking, stroking, or bruxism. At this point, rapid or unexpected movement may be interpreted as hostile gestures, leading to a feeling of paranoia.

While the higher centers of the brain are most often affected at low to moderate doses, whenever the levels reach a sufficient amount, the lower brain centers begin demonstrating effects of tremors and convulsive movements. If acute overdosage occurs, the user often reports confusion, dry mouth, dizziness, hyperreflexia, and clonicotonic convulsions. The intensity of these reactions may continue to increase and demonstrate a wide range from highly stimulated to severely depressed. The sequence of events described above has been called the "Casey Jones Reaction." There are four major concerns about the use of cocaine as it relates to this syndrome: (1) The dose at which this reaction may appear is unpredictable. The sequence of events have been set into motion with as little as 1-2 normal lines of cocaine. (2) Once the reaction begins to occur, there may only be 5 to 10 minutes during which medical intervention will be successful. (3) Even with medical intervention, this is a complex emergency. (4) Given the increase of free basing more deaths will be attributed to the Casey Jones Reaction (Gay, 1981).

In 1973, the United States government estimated that 1.5 percent of youth and 3.2 percent of adults had used cocaine. According to a recent study by the National Institute on Drug Abuse, some 14 percent of those individuals between the ages of 20 and 30 had used cocaine at least once (National Institute on Drug Abuse, 1982).

Chronic use of cocaine may result in physical exhaustion, mental confusion, anorexia, sexual impotence, visual hallucinations, delusions, and depletion of financial reserves ($1,000-$3,000 per ounce). Prolonged nasal application can cause excessive congestion and rhinorrhea (free discharge of a thin nasal mucus). "Withdrawal" symptoms include fatigue, excessive sleeping, hunger, and depression (Taylor, 1982).

"CRACK"

"Crack" is a new form of free-based cocaine being distributed throughout the United States. "Crack" first appeared during the fall of 1985. Its rise as a new form of drug abuse has been dramatic. "Crack's" trendy acceptance by the abuser population far surpasses the discovery and initial abuse of other substances such as PCP or LSD during the past twenty years. "Crack" is the street drug of the future.

The origin of the name "crack" cannot be traced to a singular individual or neighborhood. It is referred to as "rock" on the West Coast and "crack" on the East Coast. Some sellers claim the name evolved because of "crack's" close similarity to pieces of plaster which break away from tenement walls. Some users of the crystal form powder say the name comes from the crackling sound it makes when smoked. Whatever the name, it is the most potent and dangerous form of cocaine abuse in use today.

Preparation

There are two popular methods of making "crack" from cocaine HCL:

1. Cocaine HCL is mixed with **baking soda** on a 2 to 1 ratio. The mixture is then placed inside a shaker jar and water is added to make a paste. (Shaker jars are described as 3/4″ to 1″ in diameter and approximately 3″ to 4″ in height.) The paste mix is heated in the jar until dried. It is then broken into flake-like pieces and placed in a small plastic vial.

2. Cocaine is mixed with **amonia** and/or powdered amphetamine and cooked, after which the mixture is mixed with water, filtered through a cloth and allowed to dry. The crystalline-like residue is then broken up and placed in vials for marketing.

The "crack" made with amonia is reputed to give a greater euphoric effect than that made with baking soda.

Packaging

"Crack" is usually packaged in small vials. The vials are similar to over-the-counter cold or diet capsules, such as Contac® or Diet Aid® which are either clear or multicolored. Some vials are similar to those used for perfume samples.

These vials, some with plastic stoppers at one end, come in a variety of sizes and are determined to a certain degree by the distributor's access to a supply source. The vials are waterproof and may be secreted in body cavities. Other vials are made to be worn attached to necklaces or gold chains.

Prices/Weight

Prices for vials of "crack" have remained relatively stable since violators commenced distribution. The small vials, estimated to average 100 milligrams each, cost approximately $10 to $20. However, some prices for individual vials are as low as $2 to $5 each. This obviously makes "crack" an extremely affordable drug of abuse for our youth. Prices vary according to the amount of "crack" ordered, ranging from $10 to $450 for five large vials.

Purity

The purity of "crack" which the community uses ranges from 60 percent to as high as 90 percent. Based on interviews with "crack" users, a 10- to 15-minute high from a small vial appears to be average. The reaction to "crack" when smoked takes place in four to six seconds, attesting to its high purity.

Purity, without quality control, is a nebulous object. On a basis of 100 percent purity, one ounce of cocaine could provide approximately 280 vials of 100 milligram freebase.

Street Selling

About a year ago, the word "crack" was virtually unknown to street drug users. Today, however, it is a common and frequently used street word. Groups of persons have been seen "hawking" by signaling that they have "crack" to sell. "Crack" is available in locations where previously there was little or no drug activity. Most "crack" sellers report a booming business and substantial daily profits.

"CRACK SPOT"/"CRACK HOUSE"

The "crack house" is a fortified speciality dwelling established to sell "crack." A "crack spot" is a take-out only service, operated from an apartment, with a small hole drilled in the door, through which goods and money are exchanged. Abandoned buildings, storefronts, and video arcades are also used.

"BASE HOUSE"

Because freebasing requires elaborate paraphernalia, i.e., small glass pipes and a pint-size acetylene or butane torch, "base houses" have come into existence. These "base houses" are comparable to opium dens or heroin "shooting galleries." These locations are usually a club room, apartment, or similar private place. There is usually an admission charge to enter the "base house" and a separate charge for the use of a pipe and torch. The atmosphere of those places is usually quiet and serene to allow the users to relax and enjoy the drug.

Young Abusers

Today, many young persons are being turned on to "crack." Although the majority of street sellers and buyers of "crack" appear to be between

20 and 35 years old, increased teenage abuse is being noted. It is also reported that children as young as 10 or 11 years old are being introduced to "crack." Some potential drug users who would hesitate to swallow pills or use a needle would not hesitate to take a puff of a cigarette laced with cocaine base.

From Needles to "Crack"

There is a lot of talk on the street about people switching from heroin and regular cocaine to "crack." Some reasons given are a better high; no pain or needle marks; no fear of AIDS; and since "crack" is purer, the user does not worry about getting sick from a "bad cut." However, "crack" has commanded considerable law enforcement attention. As a result, many resources are being diverted from heroin locations to the newly identified "crack" locations. Some law enforcement authorities feel that heroin abusers are switching to the new free-based cocaine, but more likely, less emphasis on the continuing heroin situation naturally means less intelligence is available.

CONSEQUENCES

After-Effects

Some "crack" users reportedly become paranoid just after using it. They report hearing strange sounds or seeing things move that are not in motion; others believe people are after them and become paranoid or violent.

Addictive

The most prevailing paradox about "crack" is, "once you start using it, you cannot stop." Users speak of depleting house expenses and life savings all because of "crack." Reportedly, women have committed sex acts in base houses or turned to prostitution to get money for "crack."

Health Problems

The use of "crack" reveals that the user is vulnerable to a number of serious health-related problems. The following withdrawal symptoms have been associated with the use of "crack":

a. Worrying where to get more "crack"
b. Falling into a deep depression

c. Loss of energy and appetite

d. Difficulty in sleeping

Long-term abusers are said to lose weight, and acquire oily skin that may turn a yellow or gray tinge. Some long-term users talk of breathing problems, convulsions, and spitting up black phlegm.

Current knowledge on the effects of "crack" suggest that its effects are devastating for the user. "Crack" affects the body in the following ways:

1. Central Nervous System—Stimulation of the system produces euphoria, talkativeness, hallucinations, irritability and suspicion. Users may hallucinate and feel little insects ("cocaine bugs") crawling under the skin.

2. Arteries—Blood pressure increases 10 to 15 percent. The blood courses through the vessels at a more rapid speed and may cause, in some cases, brain hemorrhage.

3. Eyes—Pupils may dilate, becoming more sensitive to light. It may cause the abuser to think he sees "halos" surrounding objects on which he attempts to focus. The halo effect is often called "snowlights" by users.

4. Heart—Heartbeat becomes more rapid, increasing by 30 to 50 percent, and may become irregular in rare instances. It could cause a heart attack.

5. Lungs—Chronic "crack" smoking may lead to hoarseness and bronchitis, similar to the effects of marijuana or tobacco smoking.

6. Limbs—May convulse as muscles involuntarily contract.

7. Weight—May cause abusers to ignore the body's need for food and water.

Statistics

Because "crack" is a form of cocaine, arrests and seizures are lumped together in that category. Specific figures are not available at this time. Medical and treatment facilities are also feeling intense pressure from legislators and media for estimates of new admissions and for a "cure" treatment. No exact figures for admissions are available at this time.

NICOTINE

One of the most poisonous substances known to man is nicotine. Nicotine is derived from the tobacco plant and was first used by the American Indians and later exported to Europe in the fifteenth century.

Nicotine is not known to have any therapeutic value, but it has been used as an insecticide. When ingested in large doses, nicotine is toxic and even causes death. The concentration in just one cigar contains enough of the poison (120 mg.) to kill an adult if taken all at once in its pure state (Taylor, 1982).

Typically, a nonsmoker will become sick if only one cigarette is smoked. The experienced smoker, however, develops a tolerance that includes tolerance to the toxic effects of tobacco smoke. On the average, the smoke inhaled by the person smoking a cigarette contains 11.8 mg. of tar and .8 mg. of nicotine compared to 22.1 mg. of tar and 1.4 mg. of nicotine from idle smoke. Thus, the smoke from an ashtray may be twice as toxic as that inhaled by a smoker (U.S. Department of Health and Human Services, 1979). Although the concentrations inhaled by the nonsmoker are less than the concentrations inhaled by the smoker, the nonsmoker's exposure will last for a longer period. Since the discovery that the "side stream" smoke (smoke not inhaled by the smoker) is just as toxic to nonsmokers as cigarettes are to smokers, many public facilities now prohibit people from smoking.

Although controversial evidence indicates that smoking can lead to addiction to nicotine, for many individuals the habit is extremely difficult to break. Many smokers have probably attempted to quit smoking at least once, but most have failed. Freud was a classic example of dependency on this substance (20 cigars per day). He made valiant efforts to stop, but withdrawal was always too difficult. Within 30 years, Freud discovered lesions in his mouth that would not heal. These lesions were later diagnosed as being cancerous and required surgery. After some 33 operations and an artificial jaw, he still had an undiminished need to chain smoke cigars.

A smoker who gives up the habit usually experiences withdrawal syndrome. The long-term effects of nicotine (and/or tobacco smoke) can cause heart disease, gastrointestinal ailments, emphysema, and lung, mouth, and throat cancer.

Withdrawal symptoms associated with abstinence may include irritability, impatience, tremors, lack of concentration, cramps, insomnia, sweating and nervousness, decreased blood pressure, and pulse rate, compulsive overeating, intellectual impairment, and sleep disturbances. Additionally, enough nicotine can be absorbed to cause toxic effects in the infrequent user.

The new trend in tobacco use involves smokeless forms (snuff and chewing tobacco). Many users believe that this form is safe because they are not likely to develop lung cancer. While this may be true, there are other risks to which the individual is more vulnerable. Some of these include cancer of the gums, teeth, mouth, and stomach. Additionally, enough nicotine can be absorbed to cause toxic effects in the infrequent user (Taylor, 1982).

CAFFEINE

Caffeine acts on the central nervous system to elevate mood and increase wakefulness and energy. Stimulatory effects of caffeine vary from individual to individual and may vary with factors such as metabolism and personal expectation.

Caffeine is widely used throughout the United States. Reports indicate that the U.S. imports some three billion pounds of green coffee each year to satisfy the American craving for this substance. Approximately two-thirds of the caffeine, not in the form of coffee, is used in cola beverages, and the remaining one-third goes into cold remedies, headache compounds, and various nonprescription drugs.

Dependence on caffeine is primarily psychological, but individuals who regularly consume quantities of it become physiologically dependent. Mild abstinence symptoms such as anxiety, fatigue, and depression occur upon cessation of heavy use. Additionally, lowered ability to concentrate and irritability have been clearly demonstrated. Fatalities from caffeine intoxication are rare, with seven cases previously reported in the English literature. Fatalities result from respiratory arrest secondary to respiratory paralysis and seizures.

REFERENCES

Drug and Poison Information Center, University of Cincinnati, Cincinnati, Ohio, 1982.

Ellenwood, E.H., Jr. Amphetamine Psychosis I: Description of the Individuals and Process, *Journal of Neurons and Mental Disease*, 144:273-283, 1967.

Gay, George A Pharmacological Paradox, *Focus*, Vol. 5, No. 4, pp. 6, July/August, 1982.

Griffenhagen, George B. *A History of Drug Abuse*, Grassroots, January, 1972 Supplement.

Levenson, Alvin J. *Basic Psychopharmacology*, Springer Publishing Company, 1981.

Lewin, L. *Phantastica Narcotic and Stimulating Drugs*, London: Routledge and Keyan, Paul, 1964.

Peterson, Robert Cocaine—The Second Time Around, *Focus*, Vol. 5, No. 4, pp. 4, July/August, 1982.
Strachey, James Sigmund Freud: *An Autobiographical Study*, W.W. Norton and Company, Inc., 1952.
Taylor, Purcell, Jr., *Psychoactive Drugs*, Burgess Publishing Company, 1982.
U.S. Department of Health and Human Services, Public Health Services, Bibliography on Smoking and Health, *ISSN*:0067-7361, 1979.

Chapter 5

OPIOIDS

THE TERM "opioid" refers to drugs derived from the opium poppy, as well as those synthetic drugs possessing distinct chemical structures, but pharmacologically similar to mutual opium products.

The opiates are commonly used to relieve moderate to severe pain. However, despite their addictive qualities, opiods are widely prescribed and administered due to their effectiveness. Persons who use or abuse these drugs for non-medical purposes are seeking the euphoria that is so familiar with this class of drugs.

The History of Opiods

The misuse of drugs has been with us for many years. Opium is perhaps one of the first true drugs of abuse. The pleasurable uses of the opiates were described in Homer's *Iliad* as "inducing the sense of evil."

As opium addiction spread throughout China, it began to reach epidemic proportions in the early 1800's. As a result, the emperor of China issued several edicts banning the importation of opium into the country. However, despite these efforts, they proved to be generally unsuccessful. Thus, in 1839, Lin was appointed by the emperor as commissioner in charge of the opium trade abusers in Canton. Lin's first task was to demand that all Western ships storing opium surrender it immediately. However, shipping under Western control refused to surrender their cargo. In response to these violations, Lin prevented vessels from leaving port. This new approach was a big blow to Western prestige as well as to their profits. As a result, considerable tension developed between the countries involved. During a confrontation with Chinese forces over a cargo of opium, a British sailor became involved in an altercation which resulted in the death of a native Chinese. As a result, the Chinese government demanded the surrender of the British seaman involved, however, the British refused. This refusal to turn over the person involved led to the conflict known as the "Opium War of 1840-1842" (Beeching, 1975). At the conclusion of the war, the Chinese were defeated by the British. Subsequently, the British secured an indemnity against the Chinese for six million dollars and later established the port of Hong Kong (Taylor, 1982).

In America, the problem of opium addiction started before the founding of the republic. However, it was not until after the isolation of morphine that the problem of addiction was seen.

Before the passage of the Harrison Narcotics Act in 1914, the population of opiate using and dependent individuals was predominantly composed of women and the "sickly" who required the drug for pain or psychological malady. Opiates could be easily obtained by prescription or, in some cases, over the counter. Hence, systems of law enforcement, treatment, and criminal justice personnel were not required to function in relation to the use of opiates and other drugs defined as illicit. Once possession and/or sales of opiate drugs became nonsanctioned and defined as criminal, except as prescribed by physicians for specific purposes, different groups of individuals experimented with these drugs and/or became opiate dependent. After passage of the act, heroin use went underground. Heroin dependence was found in urban dwelling minority groups, often those with "bohemian" lifestyles in their late 20's and 30's. In the mid-1960's, a dramatic shift in the pattern of heroin addiction occurred. The mid- to late-teenage years became the highest risk period for those who were primarily minority-group, inner city dwellers, unemployed, single, male, high school drop-outs who frequently had a criminal history that antedated their involvement with heroin.

As drug use of all types became practically epidemic from 1965 to 1975, opiate use infiltrated all social groups across boundaries of age, gender, and race. It was reported, for instance, that up to 20 percent of U.S. servicemen stationed in Viet Nam used opiate derivatives on a regular basis. The figure 0.3 percent is accepted as the risk for the population at large. This is small in comparison to the 1 to 2 percent for the highest risk population—the medical profession (Randels, Villeponteax, Marco, Shaw, and McCurdy, 1982).

Classification of Opioids

There are several different terms used to describe opioid drugs. The term "narcotic" is the most frequently used by the addicts and the addictionologists to describe morphine-type drugs. The term "narcotic" suggests that the drug was derived from the opium poppy. Drugs in this classification may possess pharmacologic action similar to morphine or may even block the effects of morphine. Currently, there are not available classification schemes which accurately divide all of the analgesics. Thus, three separate divisions of the opioids will be reviewed in this chapter: (1) those opioids which are alkaloids of opium (2) those which mimic morphine's action at receptor sites and those which inhibit morphine-like action at others, and (3) synthetic and semisynthetic opioids.

PHARMACOLOGY

Central Nervous System Effects

The central nervous system is effected by all drugs of the opioid type. Euphoria, or the "high," rather than the mental clouding, is described by most addicts when taking opioids. However, tolerance develops rapidly to this euphoria and the individual must take an increasing amount of the drug to continue experiencing the "high" (Taylor, 1982).

The opioids' ability to react with the neuron, thus causing alteration in the release of neurotransmitters, produces pain-relieving properties. The neurotransmitters affected by these drugs thereby decreasing responses to painful stimuli, are: (1) acetylcholine, (2) norepinephrine, (3) dopamine and substance P.

In 1977, researchers discovered that the brain produced natural compounds that have opioidlike activity (Hughes and Kosterlity, 1977). These endogenous substances are commonly referred to as endorphins and enkephalins. These substances have now been discovered in other body tissue as well, i.e., the pituitary gland contains a hormone referred to as B-lipotrophin. B-lipotrophin contains a sequence of amino acids identical to B-endorphines, which successfully bind to the opioid receptor. The B-endorphins are of importance to addictionologists because when administered they can produce physical dependence and tolerance. The author believes that within the next five years our understanding of the events and circumstances surrounding these substances will lead to a much clearer understanding of addiction and dependency.

There are several other noteable actions of the opioids on the brain. The sedative effect of opiates results from depression of the sensory area of the cerebral cortex. Low or initial doses of narcotics in naive subjects stimulate the medullary chemoreceptive trigger zone (CTZ), resulting in emesis. Higher doses or repeated use results in depression of the vomiting center.

Eyes

Pupillary constriction or more accurately, overreacting to light is thought to be the result of stimulation of the Edinger-Westphal nucleus.

Mechanism of CNS Action

There is considerable interest at present in the endorphins which are polypeptide fragments of B-lipotropin in the pituitary, and which are widely distributed in the CNS. These polypeptide fragments possess opiate-like activity in several experimental systems and compete with morphine and other opiates for binding to the "opiate-receptor." Furthermore, the distribution of enkephalin binding as demonstrated by immunofluorescence, parallels fairly well the distribution of opiate receptors in the CNS. The localization of B-endorphins does not, in general, mirror the distribution of opiate receptors. Additional research needs to be done before the role of enkephalins of any of the endorphins can be established in mechanisms of pain and analgesia. At present, the evidence indicates that some endorphins may be endogenous analgesics. Like the opioids, the analgesic action seen experimentally with endorphins is reversed by naloxone.

Gastrointestinal Effects

The major effects of morphine besides its effect on the CNS is its effect on smooth muscle. In general, it causes a stimulation of smooth muscle. Opiates increase the resting tone of gastrointestinal smooth muscle, thereby slowing peristalsis, increasing the tone of the ileocecal valve and anal sphincter, and resulting in constipation (Randels, Villeponteaux, Marco, Shaw, and McCurdy, 1982).

Pancreatic Effects

Due to the intimate relationship of the biliary and pancreatic ductal systems with a frequent confluence of the two streams before entry into the duodenum, the reflux of bile into the pancreatic ductal system has been considered of etiological significance in the evolution of acute pancreatitis and perhaps chronic relapsing pancreatitis. Furthermore, the reflux of pancreatic juices into the biliary system may possibly have some effect on the gallbladder mucosa and thus perhaps result in chole-cystitis. Opioids which act upon the biliary sphincter could be of importance in producing reflux in either direction and may perhaps contribute to the development of pancreatitis or cholecystitis.

Adverse Effects

Adverse effects due to the abuse of the opioids are commonly listed in drug profiles. These include coma, shock, pinpoint pupils, depressed respiration and death by respiratory arrest.

Kidney

Morphine causes a release of ADH which decreases urine production. This effect, along with spasms of bladder sphincter and reduced "urgency" of bladder sensation, reduces frequency of urination.

Tolerance

The development of tolerance to the effects of opiates is closely associated with development of physical dependence. Notwithstanding, there are acute effects of opiates such as pupillary constriction and constipation to which the body does not become tolerant. Researchers have pointed out that alterations in the opiate receptor occur after exposure to morphine and continue to change as long as narcotics are available. Thus, they attribute tolerance to a change in quality of the receptors rather than quantity. It is well documented that, with repeated administration of opiates, both tolerance and physical dependence are established. Certainly, the organism compensates for the presence of the drug and for many of its effects, and withdrawal is a rebound phenomenon. In this context, the demonstration by Gold, Redmond, and Kleber (1978) that Clonidine®, a centrally-acting, sympatholytic antihypertensive agent, blocks opiate withdrawal symptoms is interesting.

Addiction

Psychological dependence is a factor which may develop from the use of any drug that produces pleasurable or satisfying effects. If the individual is deprived of his or her usual dose, they crave it. That is, they think that they must have the drug in order to cope with stressful or daily situations. Therefore, this craving interrupts their powers of concentration and produces agitation, anxiety, and depression. A psychologically dependent individual does not necessarily need the drug to continue to function in a "normal" manner, but he may think that he does.

When a physiologically or psychologically dependent individual abstains from the "addicting" drug, a characteristic set of withdrawal symptoms often develops. Withdrawal symptoms vary from agent to agent but may include hyperexcitability, psychomotor agitation, sweating, nausea, chills, fever, confusion, aches, anxiety, hallucinations, epileptic-like convulsions, depression, cramping, paranoid ideation, respiratory depression or arrest, heart rate irregularities, and even death. Not all agents will produce all of the above withdrawal effects. Yet, some drugs, like the CNS depressants, have withdrawal symptoms which can be life-threatening.

An individual may not only have a psychological craving for a drug, but as the body builds up a tolerance to the drug, the presence of the drug is required in order for the body to function properly or maintain homeostasis. This is not necessarily related to the amount used or frequency of use. Thus, the physiological and psychological dependency for a drug has been referred to as addiction. The reader should note that the use of the term "addiction" can mean many things to many individuals. Therefore, the reader should exercise caution when using the term. Withdrawal symptoms of a physiological nature occur upon abstinence (Taylor, 1982).

Naturally Occurring Opioids

Morphine is considered the prototype of the analgesics. Only one-fourth of raw opium contains its physiologically active chemicals called alkaloids. The dried juice (opium) contains morphine (10%) and codeine (0.5%), which are analgesic and thebaine, which is not analgesic but is related chemically. The other alkaloids in opium are not of therapeutic importance.

Morphine Withdrawal

Withdrawal can be understood on the basis of the development of tolerance. When the drug is withdrawn, the body overcompensates, or rebounds, and the opposite effect produced by opioids is seen in withdrawal. An example of this is the effect of morphine on the GI tract. Morphine causes constipation; in withdrawal, there is diarrhea. Morphine depresses the CNS, thus in withdrawal, one sees hyperactivity of the CNS. This rarely goes on to convulsions, because the original depressant effect is not that generalized.

Withdrawal from morphine and related drugs, including heroin, is rarely life-threatening, except in individuals with compromised cardiovascular function. Because of the severe diarrhea and vomiting produced in withdrawal, serious hypotension may result if fluid balance is not controlled. Opioids can be given and slowly decreased over a period of 10 days, and the withdrawal symptoms will be minimized. The former addict has no residual damage, and once withdrawn, has no physiological need for the drug. The reason few addicts ever withdraw is psychological, not physiological. Methadone® maintenance programs have been of considerable interest as a way of controlling addiction. The reasons for Methadone maintenance (i.e., taking low oral doses of Methadone daily at a Methadone clinic) are that it reduces the desire to take heroin and also decreases the sensation of pleasure if heroin is taken.

Methods of Withdrawal

The following include four distinct methods for withdrawal from the use of morphine in adults:

1. abrupt (stop all morphine-like drugs).
2. rapid (reduce dosage over a 2-3 day period until zero dose is achieved).
3. slow (reduce dosage over a 10-14 day period to zero dose).
4. substitution (stabilize on methadone and then withdraw methadone slowly).

Withdrawal Syndrome in Adults

restlessness	tremor
apprehension	headache
lacrimation	irritability
sweating	muscular weakness
chills	muscle spasm with pain
mydriasis	increased respiratory rate
diarrhea	delirium
abdominal pain	dehydration
pilomotor activity	ketosis
heart rate increase	sneezing
blood pressure increase	vomiting
yawning	anorexia

Opioid Withdrawal Symptoms in Neonates
from Addicted Mothers

Opioid withdrawal symptoms in the neonate include: (1) tremor, (2) constant head movements, (3) constant hyperactive reflexes, (4) crying, (5) excessive fluids in trachea and bronchi, (6) vomiting, (7) diarrhea, and (8) weak sucking or failure to take food.

The onset of these symptoms occurs about 48 hours to several days after birth. This is dependent on maternal opioid blood level and the type of opioid addiction before birth.

Codeine

The drugs in this class most widely used are codeine and Darvon®. Structurally, codeine is related to morphine and is obtained from opium alkaloids. The addiction liability of codeine is much less than morphine. Codeine can be prescribed without a narcotic license only in some cough syrups where the concentration of codeine is low.

Since codeine is commonly prescribed, children often acquire it from medicine cabinets and take overdoses. In codeine overdose, convulsions are often seen by the user. Severe symptoms of withdrawal are only seen when the codeine is abused injectably or when huge amounts are taken orally.

SEMISYNTHETIC AND SYNTHETIC OPIOIDS

Morphine-like Synthetic Opioids

Heroin

Heroin in its pure form is a white powder. Other colors, i.e., brown result from unsatisfactory processing of morphine or from adulterants. Heroin is usually "cut" with lactose to give it bulk and to increase profits. It has a bitter taste, and much of the time it is cut with quinine to disguise dilution.

In the U.S., heroin was first used as a cough remedy. Later, its inherent addictive properties were discovered. Whenever heroin is injected, its euphoria is greater than the experience with morphine. Heroin was banned in 1924 for use in medicine and is now considered a Schedule I drug, with a high potential for abuse.

Once in the brain, heroin is converted into morphine. Heroin carries morphine to the CNS, and intravenous heroin can be differentiated from morphine by the addict for this reason. Frequently, addicts are found dead after injecting heroin. Some of these addicts still have the needle in their vein. These deaths raise a set of important questions among professionals as to whether the person died from an unusually concentrated dose of heroin because (1) the swiftness of the person's death, (2) the low dose of heroin in most street bags, (3) the frequency of pulmonary edema involvement, and (4) the isolated nature of the phenomenon. It is more likely that death associated with heroin injection is due to concurrent use of alcohol, barbiturates, or to adulterants than it is to concentrated heroin. Probably, quinine may be the deadly adulterant in these deaths.

Heroin Withdrawal

The effects of heroin are often not pleasurable, especially after the initial dose. It is not uncommon to experience nausea and vomiting after injection. However, it should be pointed out that the euphoric effects cover up all other effects.

There are two major stages in the development of psychological dependence on heroin. These stages include: (1) a rewarding stage which includes euphoria, feelings and sensations usually pleasurable to the user. These pleasurable sensations are experienced with approximately 50 percent of the users, and (2) the user must take the drug to avoid withdrawal symptoms that will start within 12 hours after the last dose taken. These two stages are referred to as (1) primary dependence and (2) secondary psychological dependence, respectively.

After the effects of heroin disappear, the addict has approximately 4 to 6 hours to acquire additional doses of heroin before withdrawal symptoms occur. The withdrawal symptoms start with a runny nose, tears, and stomach cramps. Within 12 to 48 hours after the last dose, the addict loses all appetite, vomits, has diarrhea and abdominal cramps, with alternating chills, fever, and goose pimples all over. Between two and four days afterwards, the addict continues to experience some of the symptoms already described. In addition, the addict experiences aching bones, muscles, and powerful muscle spasms that produce violent kicking motions. After four or five days, the worst is over. It is during this period that the addict begins to clean up and initiate eating again. However, the compulsion to continue this drug-taking behavior is unchanged. The reader should keep in mind that the severity of the withdrawal syndrome may vary depending upon the following: (1) purity of the drug, (2) strength of the drug, and (3) the personality of the user (Witters and Witters, 1983).

Synthetic Opioids

Meperidine (Demerol®): Meperedine is the first of the synthetic morphine-like drugs. It was made to be "atropine-like," but actually it is "morphine-like." It is less potent, better absorbed orally, and shorter acting than morphine. Meperidine is used in obstetrics during labor. There may be less concentration of meperidine in the fetal brain than morphine, so it may depress respiration of the newborn less than morphine. Generally, all the opioid drugs cross the placenta readily. Meperidine is just as addicting as morphine.

Meperidine Withdrawal

Meperidine withdrawal is very similar to morphine withdrawal. Meperidine addicts display symptoms of withdrawal within approximately three hours after the last dose of the drug. The intensity of withdrawal symptoms from meperidine are more severe than those seen with morphine. Muscular twitching and nervousness are often more intense with meperidine. However, nausea and vomiting are less severe than seen with morphine.

Methadone

Methadone (Amidon): Methadone is a synthetic drug first produced in Germany during World War II because the Allies cut off the supplies of opium to Germany. Methadone is longer lasting, more effective orally, and has a milder withdrawal than morphine. It is used for maintenance therapy of heroin addicts and for control of withdrawal symptoms from opiates. Methadone is subject to unique restrictions because of its use in maintenance of addiction. The advantage of methadone in maintenance of addicts is that it blocks the euphorigenic effects of intravenous heroin.

Methadone Withdrawal

Symptoms of withdrawal from methadone are quite similar to those symptoms seen from morphine. These symptoms may not occur for 1 to 2 days after the drug is discontinued. Withdrawal symptoms include: (1) fatigue, (2) sluggishness, (3) vague physical complaints, and (4) irritability.

Agonist-Antagonist Opioids

An agonist drug is another name for a drug which produces a response. Heroin is considered an agonist drug because it produces a response even though this response is undesirable. An antagonist drug is a drug which blocks the agonist. Drugs such as Naloxone® (Narcan®) do not produce any response, thus they are considered to be antagonist. When a drug such as Naloxone binds strongly with a receptor, other drugs cannot then get to the receptor to produce a response.

Talwin®

Pentazocine (Talwin): This drug can be included both as an analgesic and as an antagonist to morphine-like analgesics. Since it causes neither euphoria nor dysphoria, it has less addiction potential than the other morphine-like analgesics. Its general properties are morphine-like when used as an analgesic. If given after repeated doses of morphine, Pentazocine may precipitate withdrawal signs. Although the withdrawal symptoms are milder than those of morphine, many of the symptoms are the same.

REFERENCES

Beeching, Jack *The Chinese Opium Wars*, Harcourt Brace Janvovich, New York-London, 1975.

Gold, M.S., Pottash, A.L.C., Sweeney, D.R., Kleber, H.D., Redmond, D.E. Rapid Opiate Detoxification: Clinical Evidence of Antidepressant and Antipanic Effects of Opiates, *Am. J. Psychiatry*, 136:982-983, 1979b.

Gold, M.S., Redmond, D.E., Kleber, H.D. Clonidine Blocks Acute Opiate Withdrawal Symptoms, *Lancet*, 2:599-602, 1978b.

Gold, M.S., Redmond, D.E., Kleber, H.D. Clonidine in Opiate Withdrawal, *Lancet*, 1:929-930, 1978.

Gold, M.S., Redmond, D.E., Kleber, H.D. Noradrenergic Hyperactivity in Opiate Withdrawal Supported by Clonidine Reversal of Opiate Withdrawal, *Am. J. Psychiatry*, 136:100-102, 1979.

Hughes, J., and Kasterlitz, H.W. Opioid Peptide. *British Medical Bulletin*, 1977, 33, 157-161.

Randels, P.M., Villeponteaux, L., Marco, L.A., Shaw, D.L., and McCurdy, L., *The Psychiatry Learning System*, Revised Edition, Health Sciences, Consortium, 1982.

Taylor, P. Jr., *Psychoactive Drugs*, Burgess Publishing Co., 1982.

Witters, P.J., Witters, W., *Drugs and Society: A Biological Perspective*, Wadsworth Health Sciences, 1983.

Chapter 6

HALLUCINOGENS

HALLUCINOGENIC drugs both natural as well as synthetic are substances which distort reality. These drugs have been used for centuries by various cultures and are often used in religious ceremonies. In the past 20 years, the presence of these drugs have increased dramatically, even though their dangers have been well publicized in the media.

Hallucinogens induce a state of euphoria and often cause severe depression by their action on the CNS. Thus, hallucinogens alter the normal functioning of both the CNS and the PNS. They excite the CNS causing an increase in blood pressure, body temperature, and pupil dilation. Also, the senses of time, distance, and direction become disoriented.

Hallucinogens, when consumed in large doses, often produce delusions and bizarre visual hallucinations. These effects may be either enjoyable or frightening for the drug user. Whenever the drug user experiences a frightening effect this is referred to as a "bad trip." Under these conditions, the drug user sometimes panics and is at a higher risk of injuring himself or others. Addictionologists suggest that the treatment for an anxious or panicky person under the influence of hallucinogens is to provide reassurance and comfort. Professionals often refer to this as the "talk down" (Fauman, 1981).

It should be emphasized that these drugs are unpredictable in their effects when used.

After elimination of the hallucinogen from the body, some of those who use the drug may experience a recurrence of drug effects often referred to as "flashbacks." Some flashbacks may become troublesome and unpleasant and require psychiatric evaluation and treatment. Indeed, if one under the influence was capable of becoming violent, he could also become violent in association with a flashback. However, the frequency and intensity will generally lessen with the passage of time (Taylor, 1982).

The most common hallucinogens are LSD-25, Mescaline, Psilocybin, DMT, MDA, and PCP. These substances act primarily on the central nervous system.

LYSERGIC ACID DIETHYLAMIDE

LSD is a powerful mind-altering substance capable of producing profound distortions in sight, sound, taste, and feelings in individuals. LSD was first synthesized in 1938, and its psychotomimetic effects were first discovered in 1943 when a chemist by the name of Hofmann accidentally ingested a small amount of the drug and reported its remarkable effects.

The physiological effects of LSD are extremely variable and are more or less independent of dose. The effects most commonly reported are: (1) dilation of the pupils, (2) increase in deep tendon reflexes, (3) increase in heart rate, (4) increase in blood pressure and body temperature, (5) mild dizziness or nausea, (6) chills, (7) tingling, (8) trembling, (9) slow deep respirations, (10) loss of appetite, and (11) insomnia. However, not all of these symptoms are always present in every case. In fact, the user may experience the opposite effects. LSD probably produces a broader spectrum of physical symptoms than any other drug in this class.

There have been no reported deaths due to drug toxicity with LSD. However, deaths due to accidents and suicide have frequently been reported in the literature. The three major types of adverse effects from the use of LSD are: (1) prolonged psychotic reactions, (2) acute panic reaction, and (3) flashbacks. For this reason, individuals who encourage others to use this particular drug stress the need for an appropriate setting, i.e., physical, social, and cultural. Users should be mindful that LSD is unpredictable and even the best environment and the highest conscious expectations are no guarantee against a negative experience.

LSD is generally sold in the form of tablets, thin squares of gelatin called "window panes," or imprinted paper referred to as "blotter acid." Although LSD's popularity declined during the late 1960's, there seems to be a resurgence of interest in the drug today. Only time will tell whether or not LSD will regain its place as the drug of choice in the 1980's (Young, Klein, Beyer, 1977; Greenspoon, 1979; and Brecher, 1972). The use of LSD does not lead to the development of either psychological or physical dependence. However, tolerance does develop to a high degree.

MESCALINE

Mescaline, or 3, 4, 5-trimethoxyphenylethylamine, is found in several types of cactus found in northern South America, Mexico, and the southwestern United States. Mescaline has been employed by Indians in northern Mexico from the earliest recorded time as a part of traditional religious rites. The best known is the peyote or peyote cactus. The Native American Church, which uses peyote in religious ceremonies, has been exempted from certain prosecutions of the Controlled Substances Act. Peyote, mescal buttons, and mescaline should not be confused with mescal, the colorless Mexican liquor distilled from leaves of maguey plants. The physiological and psychological effects of mescaline resemble those of LSD. In fact, individuals cannot distinguish between mescaline and LSD at appropriate dose levels in a double-blind study. Mescaline is sometimes reported to be more sensual and perceptual, with less change in the process of thinking (Taylor, 1982).

PSILOCYBIN

Like the peyote cactus, psilocybin mushrooms have been used for centuries in traditional Indian rites. Psilocybin mushrooms are found in many parts of the world, including the United States and Europe. Until recently, psilocybin mushrooms were mainly eaten in Mexico and parts of Central America where they were called by the Aztecs, teonanactl or "flesh of the gods." Although psilocybin is absorbed from the gastrointestinal tract, it often produces violent nausea and vomiting, therefore most of the ingested mushrooms are lost. The psilocybin remaining is metabolized to an inactive form in the liver, and a portion is excreted via the kidney unchanged (Kalberer, Kreis, and Rulschmann, 1962). Whenever these mushrooms are ingested, they produce mind-altering effects similar to LSD. The psychological experience is said to be more strongly visual but less intense. There seems to be more euphoria with fewer panic reactions and less paranoid reactions with this variety of the hallucinogens. In its natural form, many drug users actually prefer Psilocybin over LSD. It can now be made synthetically, but what is sold is probably adulterated.

DMT

DMT, or n, n-dimethyltryptamine, is an active ingredient in several South American plants which Indians have used for generations to create hallucinogenic effects for their religious rituals. DMT is usually combined with tobacco, parsley, or marijuana and smoked. DMT may also be ground into powder and snorted like snuff, eaten, or even prepared for injection.

DMT's effects resemble those of LSD, such as: (1) color and size, (2) visual and time distortions, (3) dizziness, and (4) a sense of alertness and clear vision. These symptoms are accompanied by sympathomimetic effects, such as: (1) dilated pupils, (2) increased blood pressure, (3) increased heart rate, and (4) increased respiration.

The greatest danger of the use of DMT is its action as an MAO inhibitor. Indeed, whenever this hallucinogen is combined with drugs such as tranquilizers, amphetamines, insulin, and alcohol and foods such as chicken, liver, and milk products, it may result in dangerous changes in vital signs resulting in death.

MDA

MDA, or 3, 4-Methylenedioxyamphetamine, is a drug that has been available on the illicit market since 1967. MDA's effects do not resemble those which have already been discussed previously. MDA produces feelings of esthetic delight, joy, insight, and serenity without perceptual distortions or loss of control. MDA seems to be capable of relieving anxiety and defensiveness. Users have reported reliving childhood memories while remaining aware of present self and surroundings. The user also feels affectionate and wants to be close to individuals in an effort to break through human boundaries.

MDA seems to be more preferred on the illicit market than LSD and the other drugs because it distorts reality less and produces fewer harmful emotional effects. However, at considerably higher doses (150 to 200 mg.), some users have reported LSD-like effects. Due to the fact that MDA is produced in clandestine laboratories, it is rarely pure, and the dose, regardless of its form should be expected to vary considerably. There have been several reported deaths as a result of the ingestion of MDA. However, these reports should be suspect because of the possibility of the drug being contaminated by other drugs on the illicit market.

PCP

Phencyclidine (PCP), is a powerful psychedelic that, according to professionals, poses greater risk to the user than any other drug of abuse. PCP was patented in 1963 as a surgical analgesic and anesthetic under the name of Sernyl®. However, PCP was banned from use on humans in 1965 because of delirium, agitation, and disorientation reported after emergency from anesthesia following surgery. If it were not for its ability to produce psychotic behavior, PCP could become a useful adjunct to surgeons. The rational given for this, is because, unlike other general anesthetics, PCP does not produce fatal medullary responses.

In 1967, PCP was marketed under the name of Sernylan® as an animal tranquilizer and anesthetic. PCP appeared on the illicit market the same year under various names such as "Rocket Fuel," "Angel Dust," "Embalming Fluid," and "Super Weed." PCP is also often misrepresented as mescaline, psilocybin, THC, or LSD. Phencyclidine is usually seen as a white crystalline powder which can be taken orally, intravenously, or snuffed. Generally, PCP is sprinkled on marijuana or parsley leaves and smoked. However, because most PCP is made in clandestine laboratories, it contains contaminants resulting in a change of color ranging from tan to brown, causing the user to think that it is one of the other psychedelic drugs.

The behavioral effects of PCP are remarkable. Users of this drug report the following effects: (1) sense of detachment, (2) distance, (3) physical and emotional numbness, (4) floating sensations, (5) feeling of emotional or sensory isolation, (6) changes in body image and space, (7) loss of coordination, (8) sense of strength and invulnerability. Psychosis indistinguishable from schizophrenia may occur and continue as little as a few hours or as long as two weeks. Psychosis is followed by partial or total amnesia for the period since taking the drug. Although these reactions are generally associated with repeated use of the drug, psychosis has been known to occur with only a single dose and the effects last long after the drug has been excreted from the body.

The chronic use of PCP is becoming widespread throughout the United States and its overall effects have not been adequately studied. However, agressive behavior and specific incidences of violence usually committed by chronic users have been reported. Physical addiction in the classic fashion does not occur, however, compulsive involvement with the drug is well documented. There have been several deaths from drowning, hypertensive crisis, results of violence, and similar incidences reported by professionals.

CANNABIS

There has never been a drug used that is more shrouded in mystery and misconception than marijuana. Cannabis' active ingredient, tethrahydrocannabinal (THC), was synthesized in 1966. In Arabia, it is known as "hashish," still carrying with it the lurid tales of Hasan and Assassins, who were credited with performing the most death-defying deeds under its influence.

In India, cannabis has been cultivated as a drug for thousands of years. The potency of the hemp resides in the sticky and aromatic resin which coats the female flowers. The most potent of all of the hemp is the "charas" which is produced in Central Asia.

In Bombay, the "charas" is incorporated into a sweetmeat called "maajun," which is popular among women. In Algeria, a special delicacy is made from cannabis by grinding the hemp tops with sugar, cinnamon, orange juice, cloves, cardamom, nutmeg, musk, pistachios, and pine kernels and forming it into small candy patties. Some orientals claim that by adding a pinch of knocks vomica or cantharides, it will increase aphrodisiac effects (NIMH, 1972).

However, the main form of cannabis use is by inhalation. The smoke of the marijuana cigarette contains about 5 to 7.5 mg. of THC of which only part is absorbed by the user. Hashish is about 5 to 10 times more potent than marijuana.

Throughout the Far East, hashish is smoked in special pipes called "josies." When the Egyptian government restricted the use of hashish, the users turned to other sources of supply, i.e., smuggling.

The problem of cannabis in the United States is relatively new. Cannabis is believed to have been first introduced in the United States by Mexican laborers. The habit of smoking marijuana grew in the New Orleans area and was soon seen all over the country as thousands of pounds of the drug were smuggled in. Later, lurid stories began to appear in the news media of the effects of the drug. Reports ranged from increased talkativeness to unpremeditated acts of violence.

Today, the subject of cannabis continues to stimulate controversy and lively debate. Proponents of the drug argue that cannabis is one of the safest social intoxicants available if it is used in a responsible manner. Opponents believe that cannabis is not an innocuous substance, and that it does have some serious adverse effects.

What does the current scientific evidence provide on the possible risk individuals take when they use cannabis? In an effort to assess the evidence, we will explore nine different areas concerning effects from the use of cannabis (Pollin, 1981).

1. Brain Damage Research

Currently, it is not possible to make definitive statements concerning the relationship between cannabis use and brain damage. In the past several years, investigators have indicated possible brain atrophy might be present in the frequent users of cannabis. However, one must point out that these studies have serious methodological flaws that prevent making any concrete conclusions. Also, no proof exists that cannabis produces any specific neurologic illness. Some investigators have observed paranoid reactions, hallucinations, decreased tolerance to pain and precipitation of psychosis in prepsychotic individuals that use cannabis. Thus far, these studies have not been confirmed by others. Additional research in this area is needed, specifically regarding the subtle changes in brain functioning that may occur as a result of cannabis use.

2. Chromosome Abnormalities

Currently, there exists no definite proof that cannabis use causes clinically significant chromosome damage in humans. Although earlier research studies indicate increases in chromosomal abnormalities in human cell cultures, more recent studies appear to be contradictory.

3. Pulmonary Effects

There is a greater risk for cancer associated with frequent heavy use of cannabis. The increased risk of cancer is probably due to the high percentage of cannabis tar which contains over 150 complex hydrocarbons including carcinogens such as benzo(a)pyrene. The concentration of benzo(a)pyrene in cannabis tar is 70 percent higher than in the same weight of tobacco tar. Currently, no animal model exists for the development of lung cancer by cannabis or tobacco. However, longitudinal studies are now being supported by the National Institute on Drug Abuse to evaluate the long-term risks of cannabis. In addition to cancer risk, cannabis smoke has been shown to cause increased resistance to air flow because of its irritant properties. This leads to adverse effects such as laryngitis, sore throat, and bronchitis in those who are frequent heavy users of the drug. At this time, it is difficult to predict precisely the health hazards in later life among those young people who are regular cannabis users. As with cigarette smoking, it may take many years to fully document the results.

4. Immune Response

Impairment of immune responses and alterations in certain hormone levels have been reported. However, there has been no large-scale epidemiological research studies conducted to determine if cannabis smokers suffer from infections and other diseases to a greater extent than individuals of similar life styles who do not use cannabis.

5. Psychopathology

Our current knowledge of the psychological and psychiatric effects of cannabis is limited. Young people are believed to be especially vulnerable because of their on-going physical and emotional maturation. Due to this fact, there is increasing clinical concern that heavy daily use of cannabis may produce psychological dependence to such an extent that it may interfere significantly with the maturation of adolescents. Some commonly observed adverse clinical reactions to cannabis use are acute anxiety reaction, paranoid states, and psychotic decompensation. Another clinical reaction to cannabis is acute brain syndrome, which includes: (1) clouding of mental process; (2) disorientation; (3) confusion and marked memory impairment. These symptoms seem to be related to both the dosage and the quality of cannabis used. Difficulty occurs in determining the role cannabis plays in psychopathology due to other potential contributing variables such as normal developmental crises, other drugs, and latent psychopathology.

6. Reproductive Effects

Studies of both animals and humans suggest that daily use of cannabis in substantial amounts may impair certain aspects of the reproductive function. Several studies indicate that the male hormone testosterone may be decreased temporarily as a result of heavy cannabis use. Abnormalities in sperm count, motility, and structural characteristics of sperms have been found in males who are long-term users of cannabis. Preliminary evidence suggests that heavy cannabis use ranging from several times per week to daily use may decrease fertility in women. However, these effects may be reversible when cannabis use is discontinued. Recent animal studies using high doses of cannabis of THC indicate a variety of potential reproductive problems. These include: (1) early death of embryos and their reabsorption, (2) lower birth weight, (3) reduction in ovary and uterine weight, (4) reduced estrogen production, and (5) reduced production of several important pituitary hormones. When cannabis is used during pregnancy, the expectant mother should be aware that the active ingredient, THC, crosses the placenta and enters the fetus' circulation. THC may also be passed on to the newborn by way of the mother's breast milk. Although research concerning the effects of cannabis on human reproduction is limited, one must emphasize that the evidence at least warrants warnings against the frequent use of cannabis during pregnancy.

7. Cardiovascular Effects

Cannabis use is known to lead to increased heart rate and associated circulatory changes. There exists some evidence that suggests that individuals with impaired heart function may precipitate angina pectoris more rapidly than with tobacco cigarettes. These observations may prove to be an important medical discovery in individuals under 21 who presently use cannabis as they progress through middle life.

8. Driving Skills

There is considerable evidence that cannabis impairs driving ability. Studies involving the perceptual components of driving skills, driver simulator performance test course and actual driving ability all tend to illustrate significant performance and perceptual deficits related to being "high." Many more cannabis users drive today when "high" than ever before. Studies conducted by the National Highway Traffic Safety Administration indicates that cannabis probably was used by a significant number of drivers involved in fatal accidents. Also, the use of cannabis in combination with alcohol is quite common. The risk of auto accidents when these two drugs are combined poses a greater risk than when either drug is used alone. Studies are now being conducted to quickly detect cannabinoids in body fluids such as saliva and blood to confirm use or nonuse within the recent past.

9. Intellectual Functioning

There has been a wide range of intellectual impairments related to cannabis intoxification reported. Deficits have been reported in such tasks as: (1) digit symbol substitution, (2) reaction time, (3) the ability to repeat digits backward and forward, (4) speech impairment, (5) concept formation, (6) reading comprehension, and (7) the ability to transfer information from immediate to long-term memory storage. Research consistently shows that while cannabis' acute effects on memory and cognition may vary depending on the task and the amount of drug used, the results invariably are detrimental. However, additional research in this area is still needed.

Investigation on the medical benefits of THC are still being studied. However, some potential therapeutic uses have been reported in the past several years. These benefits include: (1) the prevention of nausea and vomiting which accompanies chemotherapy in cancer patients, (2) the use as a bronchodilator in patients with asthma, (3) the treatment of some convulsive disorders, and (4) the treatment of certain eye disorders by reducing fluid pressure in the eyes.

REFERENCES

Brecher, Howard and the Editors of Consumer Reports, *Licit and Illicit Drugs*, Little Brown and Company, Boston, 1972.

Fauman, Beverly S., and Fauman, Michael A., *Emergency Psychiatry for the House Offices*, William and Wilkins, Baltimore, 1981.

Finch, Bernard, *Passport to Paradise*, Philosophical Library, New York, 1960.

Greenspoon, Lester and Bakalai, James B., *Psychedelic Drugs Reconsidered*, Basic Books, Inc., New York, 1979.

Pollin, William M.D., Director NIDA, Health and Educational Effects of Marijuana on Youth, Statement given before the Sub-committee on Alcoholism and Drug Abuse, Committee on Labor and Human Resources, United States Senate, October 21, 1981.

Student Association for the Study of Hallucinogens, National Clearing House for Drug Abuse Information, National Institute of Mental Health, U.S. Department of Health, Education, and Welfare, 1972.

Young, Klein, and Beyer, *Recreational Drugs*, Collier-McMillan Publishers, 1977.

Kalberer, F., Kreis, W., and Rulschmann, Jr., The Fate of Psilocin in the Rat. *Brochemical Pharmacology*, April/May 1962, 11, 261-269.

Chapter 7

PSYCHOPHARMACOLOGY

THE INTRODUCTION of the psychopharmacological therapies occurred during the 1950's. They largely eliminated the more drastic forms of medical treatment for emotional conditions believed incurable. Although it was known for many years that drugs influence behavior, it was not until recently that psychotherapeutic agents were used in treating maladaptive behavior.

Anxiety

Anxiety may be thought of as intense apprehension and fear. Anxiety often occurs without any apparent cause that is accompanied by physical changes such as increased heart rate, sweating, physical pain, diarrhea, nausea, vomiting, etc.

A classification of drugs known as the benzodiazepines are effective agents for many of the physiologic as well as the psychologic symptoms of anxiety. Their site of action involves the benzodiazepine receptors found in the brain that function to potentiate the effects of gamma-amino-butyric acid (GABA). Researchers have discovered that GABA is found in every synapse investigated. Researchers have also found that GABA function is inhibitary, i.e., the postsynaptic cell responds by reducing output of nerve impulses.

In 1977, a specific benzodiazepine receptor was discovered. This receptor lies next to a GABA receptor and the chloride channel in the cell membrane. The arrangement of these receptors is often referred to by psychopharmacologists as the super moleclar receptor complex (SMRC). Whenever a benzodiazepine is administered, it binds with the benzodiazepine receptor in the brain causing a series of events to occur within the cell membrane itself. When GABA occupies the GABA receptor, there is a conformational shift in the GABA receptor which in turn increases the probability that the chloride channel will open. The channel can be visualized as a hole in the membrane which is either closed or open. Normally, the chloride channel is closed. Whenever the chloride channel opens, chloride ions move from the outside of the cell to the inside. The cell then becomes more negatively charged and is more difficult to excite. GABA has greater success in opening the chloride channel when the benzodiazepine receptor is occupied. The reader should keep in mind that it is this system the SMRC which is believed most or all of the anxiolytics work.

The reader may be asking why did this benzodiazepine receptor evolve in nature. Certainly, it was not to anticipate the discovery of drugs by pharmaceutical companies. Rather, there must be some reason from an evolutionary perspective why this receptor developed. Recent research suggests that the site of this system is where generalized anxiety is initiated. However, exactly how this occurs is not fully known at this time.

The anxiolytics, or antianxiety agents, are prescribed for well-defined situational stresses which cannot be effectively handled any other way. More specifically, they are used for neurotic disorders, anxiety, nervousness, muscle relaxation, alcohol withdrawal, seizure disorders, and other neurological problems.

CLASSIFICATION OF ANXIETY

Anxiety

Primary Anxiety

Anxiety States:
  Panic Disorder
  Generalized Anxiety Disorder
  Obsessive-Compulsive Disorder
  Posttraumatic Stress Disorder

Phoebic Disorders
  Agoraphobia
  Social Phobia
  Simple Phobia

Situational Anxiety

1. Major Medical Disorder
2. Substance Abuse
3. Major Psychiatric Disorder
4. Psychosocial Stressors

Side Effects

In most individuals, an anti-anxiety effect can be achieved with very few adverse effects. The most common side effects reported are fatigue, sleepiness, muscle weakness, dizziness, and disturbances of coordination. Tolerance to the sedative effects of the benzodiazepines will usually occur within several days of administration.

Other adverse side effects include nausea and other gastrointestinal complaints, hiccups, constipation, increased appetite, anorexia, weight gain or loss, dry mouth, and decreased libido.

A paradoxical CNS stimulation has been reported occasionally with benzodiazepines. Symptoms such as talkativeness, restlessness, anxiety, euphoria, tremulousness, sleep disturbances, excitement, and hyperactivity have occurred, usually early in the course of therapy. Excitation is most likely to occur in psychiatric patients and in hyperactive, aggressive children.

Toxicity

Due to the large differences between the effective and lethal doses of benzodiazepines, it is unlikely that ingestion of acute overdose will be fatal unless other CNS depressants are also ingested. Overdose with benzodiazepines can result in somnolence, confusion, coma, and diminished reflexes. Any intentional overdose of benzodiazepines should be taken seriously and medical treatment should be obtained because of the likelihood that other drugs may be involved.

Tolerance and Physical Dependence

One possible explanation for the development of tolerance is that there is a gradual decrease in the number of GABA receptors to compensate for continued GABA inhibition. The withdrawal illness that occurs when the benzodiazepine is discontinued is caused by the insufficiency of neural inhibition when the drug is absent. The withdrawal illness disappears when the neurons synthesize new GABA receptors.

Withdrawal illness is clearly associated with prolonged use of high doses of the benzodiazepines. There are more and more reports of withdrawal illness associated with prolonged use of normal dosages of benzodiazepines and mild withdrawal illness associated with even several months use of normal dosages.

Mild withdrawal from the use of these drugs (anxiety, insomnia, and tremor) closely mimic idiopathic anxiety, causing a vicious cycle of use and reinforcing psychological dependence. Withdrawal symptoms include dysphoria, sensory changes, hyperreflexia, diaphoresis, tremor, and agitation. Seizures have been reported following withdrawal of benzodiazepines. Benzodiazepines should never be abruptly discontinued, after chronic use (also, the gradual reduction in dosage will prevent the emergence of significant withdrawal reactions).

Use in Pregnancy

In retrospective studies, results suggest an increased risk of congenital malformations in infants of mothers who receive benzodiazepines (diazepam, chlordiazepoxide, and oxazepam) during the first trimester of pregnancy. Administration of these drugs during labor and delivery can produce serious CNS depression in the newborn. Additionally, infants of mothers who chronically ingested benzodiazepines during pregnancy have been reported to have withdrawal symptoms. Therefore, the use of these drugs during the first trimester of pregnancy should almost always be avoided.

Neuroleptics

The use of antipsychotic drugs referred to as neuroleptics are in the view of many clinicians the most significant advance in the treatment of psychopathology. The term "antipsychotic" is appropriate, because all neuroleptics influence favorably the result of CNS derangement, toxic insult, or functional disorders. Schizophrenias are the most common type of psychosis, hence the term "antischizophrenic" is often used to describe these agents.

The discovery of the phenothiazines opened a new era of chemotherapy for the mentally ill. These drugs are now widely used to treat schizophrenia, destructive behavior, delirium, mania, hallucinations, paranoia, and confusion.

The three phenothiazines that will be considered here are: chlorpromazine (Thorazine®), fluphenazine (Prolixin®), and thioridazine (Mellaril®). The therapeutic effects of these drugs are somewhat similar. However, they differ in unwanted effects as well as dosage. Chlorpromazine and thioridazine have predominantly a complex of side effects consisting of hypotension, sedation, and anticholinergic signs, while fluphenazine has predominantly extrapyramidal side effects. The exact mechanism of these drugs' therapeutic effects is not clear at this time, however, it is thought to be related to the dopamine blocking action that they exert at the central receptor sites (Wyatt, 1976; Meltzer, Stahl, 1976).

The antipsychotic drugs have the capacity to eliminate delusions, hallucinations, psychomotor agitation, and to restore contact with reality. This capacity to diminish or restore the disordered thought processes is what makes the antipsychotics so valuable in the alleviation of psychotic behavior (Taylor, 1982). Pharmacologically, all effective neuroleptics block dopamine activity in varying degrees. Recent research indicates that the schizophrenic brain has twice the number of normal dopamine receptors.

Although the neuroleptics are not addicting, they all possess the ability to produce adverse side effects. The most prominent side effects are the anticholinergic and the extrapyramidal effects. The anticholinergic effects include blurred vision, dry mouth, constipation, and urinary retention.

NEUROLEPTIC INDUCED EXTRAPYRAMIDAL REACTIONS

Early Onset

1. Acute dystonia, akathisia, or parkinsonism
2. Appears within first 10 weeks of treatment
3. Causes distress
4. Helped by:
   Anticholinergic medication
   Decreasing dose of antipsychotic
5. Always reversible

Late Onset

1. Tardive dyskinesia
2. Appears after a minimum of 3 months of treatment — usually after years
3. Causes no distress
4. Worsened by:
   Anticholinergic medication
   Decreasing dose of antipsychotic
5. Often irreversible

What Is Tardive Dyskinesia?

Tardive dyskinesia is a neuroleptic-induced neurological disorder which stands apart from other extrapyramidal syndromes induced by neuroleptic compounds.

Tardive dyskinesia is the most tragic and frightening consequence of long-term use of neuroleptic compounds. It is becoming a major public health issue. The true incidence is not known at this time. However, estimates range from 5 to 50 percent of those who are chronic drug patients. Tardive dyskinesia is the name used for certain abnormal movements of the mouth, tongue, face, arms, legs, and body. These movements cannot be stopped by the individual at will for a considerable length of time. They can be momentarily stopped at will. Some individuals may have only minor lip smacking, tongue movements, or facial movements. However, others may have severe movements that interfere with eating, talking, and walking. The individual appearance may become so distracting and bizarre that the person becomes socially isolated from others. Movements become worse whenever the person becomes tense or anxious, and become better when the person is calm.

Due to the fact that there is no adequate treatment for tardive dyskinesia, the only definite treatment is the withdrawal of the neuroleptics (often referred to as a "drug holiday") extending over a period of several weeks during a year. However, more frequent "drug holiday" intervals may prevent the occurrence of these parkinson-like symptoms.

Other side effects include cardiac toxicity, skin rashes, retinal pigmentation, photosensitivity, weight gain, toxic retinopathy, and sudden death (reported very rarely).

Antidepressants

Depression is a mood disorder which is characterized by severe and prolonged feelings of despair, hopelessness, low self-esteem, and self-blame. In the early 1900's, electroconvulsive shock therapy (ECT) was the treatment of choice in cases of severe depression (Adams, 1981). Today, a greater number of clinicians are prescribing antidepressant drugs in the treatment of depression. These drugs may take anywhere from two to three weeks to become effective after therapy is begun. Of greater importance is the fact that the population for which these drugs are the most effective is also the population with the highest risk for suicide. Thus, it is important that these individuals be closely monitored while using these drugs (Taylor, 1982).

Tricyclics

Among the antidepressant drugs, the tricyclics are the most commonly prescribed for the treatment of depression.

Indications for Tricyclic Use

1. Endogenous — Depression
2. Manic Depression — Depressive Phase
3. Depression with Anxiety and/or Agitation
4. Reactive Depression (Treatment of Choice is Psychotherapy)
5. Childhood Bedwetting (Imipramine® used for children)
6. Narcolepsy (Protriptyline and Imipramine are used)

Side Effects of Tricyclic Antidepressants

The side effects of tricyclic antidepressants are: (1) anticholinergic, (2) sedative, (3) cardiovascular, and (4) other.

1. Anticholinergic Side Effects

Dry mouth, difficulty urinating, and blurred vision.

2. Sedative Side Effects

a. Most Sedating TCA's — Doxepin and Amitriptyline
b. Less Sedating — Nortriptyline and Desipramine
c. Energizing — Protriptyline (may cause insomnia)

3. Cardiac Side Effects

Cardiac Side Effects Include:
(1) Orthostatic Hypotension — When abruptly standing, after being in a
sitting or lying position, the blood pressure drops drastically. This may
result in injury due to falls. This side effect is more commonly seen in
elderly patient's taking tricyclic antidepressants, (2) Rapid Heart
Rate — May precipitate angina in patients with coronary artery disease, (3) Prolonged Intraventricular Conduction — May cause ventri-
cular fibrillation leading to sudden death, (4) Decreased Conduction
Velocity — May cause heart block in patients with a compromised conduction system, and (5) The tricyclic antidepressants also have an anti-
arrhythmic property.

4. Other Side Effects

(1) Weight Gain — Increased craving for sweets, (2) Photosensitivity —
Although not common with the tricyclics, sunburn may be avoided by
using a good sunscreen, (3) Blood Disorders — Note constant sore
throat, fever, yellow skin or eyes, and (4) Aggravated Glaucoma —
Note eye pain.

MAOI

Another class of antidepressants used less frequently than the tricyclic antidepressants are the monoamine oxidase inhibitors (MAOI). These drugs are usually prescribed after unsuccessful therapeutic trials of the tricyclics. These drugs also have troublesome side effects such as mania, liver damage, and hypertensive crisis.

Evidence is available which suggests that depression is the result of insufficient brain levels of the transmitter norepinephrine or deficiencies in serotonin, another transmitter (Schildkraut, 1965, 1973). Thus, both the tricyclics and the MAO inhibitors serve us well by increasing the levels of these neurotransmitter substances.

Lithium

Lithium is a special agent for the treatment of bipolar affective disorders. Lithium is the treatment of choice for acute manic episodes. The reason why lithium is the choice is (1) it acts to normalize mood, (2) it does not excessively sedate, (3) it may prevent future manic episodes, and (4) it is not addictive. Lithium effects are observed after several days of treatment. The drug relieves manic symptoms without sedation or the feeling of being drugged, and moderates the larger mood swings of bipolar affective disorders. However, because of its slow action, lithium is not used alone in the management of the acute manic phase (Mendels, 1976). The neuroleptics are used adjunctively to control hyperactivity and insomnia.

Most individuals require from 1200-1800 mg. of lithium per day to achieve effective levels of the drug. The side effects of lithium include vomiting, diarrhea, increased thirst, nausea, muscle weakness, a diabetes insipidus-like syndrome, electrocardiogram changes, skin rashes, edema, and nontoxic goiter (Taylor, 1982).

REFERENCES

Adams, Henry E. *Abnormal Psychology*, Wm. C. Brown, 1981.

Maas, J.W. Biogenic Amines and Depression: Biochemical and Pharmacological Separation of Two Types of Depression, *Arch. Gen. Psychiat.*, 26:252-262, 1972.

Maas, J.W., Fawcett, J.A., and Dekirmenjiam, H. Catecholamine Metabolism, Depressive Illness, and Drug Response, *Arch. Gen. Psychiat.*, 26:252-262, 1972.

Meltzer, H. and Stahl, S. The Dopamine Hypothesis of Schizophrenia: A Review, *Schizophrenia Bulletin*, 2, 1976.

Mendels, J, Stern, S., and Frazer, A. Biochemistry of Depression, *Dis. Nerv. Syst.*, 37:3-9, 1976.

Schildkraut, J.J. The Catecholamine Hypothesis of Affective Disorders: A Review of Supporting Evidence, *Amer. J. Psychiat.*, 122:509-522, 1965.

Schildkraut, J.J. Norepinephrine Metabolites as Biochemical Criteria for Classifying Depressive Disorders and Predicting Responses to Treatment: Preliminary Findings, *Amer. J. Psychiat.*, 130:695-698, 1973.

Taylor, P. Jr., *Psychoactive Drugs*, Burgess Publishing Company, 1982.

Wyatt, R.J. Biochemistry and Schizophrenia (Part IV): The Neuroleptics, Their Mechanism of Action: A Review of the Biochemical Literature, *Psychopharmacological Bulletin*, 12:5-50,1976.

Chapter 8

DECLARE THERAPY: NEW DIRECTIONS IN THE TREATMENT OF SUBSTANCE ABUSE

INTRODUCTION

THE AUTHOR is currently conducting experimental research into a new technique which seems to hold promise in the treatment of chemical dependency. The purpose of this research is to develop a specific more efficiently oriented treatment process that is short-term and multimodal in the treatment of chemically dependent individuals. Strictly speaking, additional research needs to be conducted to substantiate the validity and usefulness of the principles and concepts of this approach with various populations.

Over the past several decades a number of therapeutic approaches have been employed in attempting to understand the nature of both physiological and psychological factors in the development of mental disorders. The role of these therapies is complex and varied in terms of their application to substance abuse disorders. Thus, drug abusers as well as those who are chemically dependent have been traditionally treated by therapeutic approaches which were not specifically designed for them. Consequently, approaches such as psychoanalysis, cognitive restructuring, behavioral (operant) conditioning, and psychopharmacology present problems for both drug clients and therapists alike because of their underlying belief systems.

The following are not meant to cast disparagement on any contributions made by a particular approach, nor is it meant to minimize their significance in shaping the fields of psychology or psychiatry. On the contrary, the only purpose here is to point out the limitations of these approaches in their use with chemically-dependent individuals.

At this junction, it may be of importance for the reader to look at some of the limitations of the various therapeutic approaches used in the treatment of the substance abuse disorders.

Psychoanalytical Techniques

Despite a popular acceptance of psychiatric therapy, there remains a gnawing professional suspicion that these treatment methods leave much to be desired, with neither the process or the outcome well defined (Spitzer and Klein, 1976).

Generally, those disposed to use this method emphasize the development of emotional insight and understanding into the relationship between intrapsychic process and overt behavior (Freud, 1924). In other words, the primary goal of psychoanalytic counseling is for the client to achieve insight into intrapsychic or unconscious conflicts. For instance, the substance abuser must come to realize that the instinctual impulses of childhood which overwhelmed the ego were distorted by his superego and that these are now manifested in his/her later behavior (e.g., substance abuse). Other limitations of this technique are (1) too expensive, (2) too intellectual to be useful in dealing with nonmiddle-class people, (3) not enough trained professionals to offer one-to-one therapy to all persons who want or need it, and (4) the effectiveness or benefits of psychodynamic therapy is questionable (Szasz, 1961 and Williams, 1976).

Cognitive Techniques

Second, the use of cognitive restructuring approaches pose certain limitations in the treatment of the substance abuse disorders. Briefly, cognitive restructuring techniques emphasize the idea that emotional reactions result mainly from the evaluative thoughts, attitudes, and beliefs an individual ascribes to a given situation, the way individuals think about things cause them to create their own emotional, physical, and behaviorial responses. Therefore, in order to change behavior, those attitudes that give rise to, support, or reinforce behavior by necessity need to be changed (Pervin, 1980).

Therefore, the main purpose of the therapist in cognitive restructuring is to help the client identify irrational or self-defeating beliefs and to point out to the client how to dispute these, self-defeating beliefs and teach him or her how to replace them with more rational self-enhancing beliefs.

An obvious limitation of this approach is that emotional difficulties tend to be associated with specific irrational ideas. Thus, the cognitive restructuring theorists do not address directly the emotional aspects which often contribute to the global picture of the substance abuser. Generally speaking, additional research needs to be conducted to substantiate the validity and usefulness of the concepts and principles of cognitive restructuring techniques.

Phenomenological Techniques

Third, the phenomenological approach emphasizes the unequalness of humans in general and each person in particular. Thus, its orientation provides comfort and reassurance that people are not just a quantitative extension of someone or something else. In addition, it is an optimistic approach which focuses on the positive potentials in human life. Finally, it places faith and trust in the person's capability to grow toward complete fulfillment of his/her ultimate experiential and behavioral capacities.

The limitations of the phenomenological approach are: (1) Its approach is too narrowly concerned with immediate conscious experience. Thus, it pays little or no attention to the significance in determining behavior of unconscious origins, reinforcement contingencies, situational influences, and biological factors, etc. (2) It does not adequately address the development of human behavior. (3) It provides excellent descriptions of behavior, but it is usually not focused on the scientific exploration of its functional cause (Truax, 1966).

To suggest that people act as they do because of some unique perceptions of reality may be satisfying, but this is not very informative in terms of promoting understanding of the variables operating to develop, maintain, and alter behavior. (4) Phenomenological concepts are unscientific, vague, esoteric, and in general, difficult to comprehend, let alone research. (5) Its theories are anti-intellectual and antiscientific. In this approach, reason is subordinated to feelings. Also, knowledge is sought through subjective experience rather than rational analysis. (6) Its clinical applicability is limited to those segments of the population whose intellectual, educational, and cultural background are compatible with the introspective nature of this approach. Individuals who are not in this somewhat select group may find that the theories of this approach make little sense.

Behavioral Techniques

Fourth, the behaviorist conception of counseling are mostly concerned with psychological variables that lend themselves easily to observations, measuring, and recording. Therefore, treatment is based on behaviorial analysis of covert processes, such as thoughts and emotions as far as they can be reliably recorded. Thus, the goal of behaviorial counseling has to do with changing the reinforcing conditions that support maladaptive behavior or the situation which elicits it. The focus therefore is on specific response-reinforcement processes rather than on abstract and general psychological ones.

Some limitations of this approach are: (1) Behavioral perspective tends to ignore genetic, physiological, constitutional, and other nonlearning-based influences. The learning approach also fails to emphasize sufficiently the significance of subjective experience and each individual's unique potential for positive growth. (2) It is only applicable to that narrow range of human activity in which behavior is measurable. It does not adequately conceptualize or ameliorate human problems of a complex internal nature. (3) All learning principles are not clearly established and animal-laboratory results may not allow clinicians to meaningfully apply these principles to the behavior of human beings. Thus, a dog faced with an insolvable task might display "experimental neurosis," but the human behavior referred to as "neurotic" may not be equivalent and may result from entirely different processes. (4) Social-learning approaches are not as clearly validated or scientific as behaviorists would have us think. Many of the assessment and treatment procedures in social learning are based more upon clinical experience than on experimental research. Also, where there is research evidence, it is most often not unequivocally supportive of learning-based techniques (Kenfer and Karaly, 1972; Herrnstein, 1977 and Taylor, 1963).

Psychopharmacological Techniques

Finally, psychopharmacology is one of the newer clinical approaches used in the treatment of substance abuse disorders. Basically, this approach concerns itself with the major clinical syndromes and the manner in which the sciences of pharmacology may be useful, either immediately or ultimately, in their cure. Some limitations of this technique include (1) a high potential for abuse, (2) drugs alter social behavior, (3) drugs may interfere in the therapeutic process, (4) drugs may produce undesirable (toxic) side effects, (5) drugs may be used to control individuals, i.e. what Thomas Szasz refers to as "chemical strait jackets," (6) drugs may be used to exploit patients who desire a quick relief from psychic distress, and (7) drugs often influence the thinking and behavior of both client and therapist (Szasz, 1961).

As a clinician using therapeutic modalities such as psychoanalysis and behaviorism in the treatment of substance abuse disorders, the author has become increasingly aware of the limitations of these approaches.

As a result of these limitations, an attempt was begun to define principles and develop a method and technique that would make possible a shorter more efficiently oriented treatment process. Declare Therapy is the result of this effort, however, it is not a panacea. It is meant to be a short-term focal, experientially based, multimodal approach for the treatment of chemically dependent individuals. Through this approach, the substance abuser learns to minimize undesirable behavior (drug taking) and maximize desirable (refraining from abusing drugs) behavior through a multimodal therapeutic approach.

Psychosocial Stages of Drug Abuse/Individual and Family

In counseling drug dependent persons and their families, the author has recognized a series of seven psychosocial stages related to their acceptance, treatment and entry back into society for drug dependent problems. The author has designated these seven psychosocial trait stages by each of the seven letters in the word D.E.C.L.A.R.E.. The rationale for this decision took into account that a person must admit to himself or herself that significant others i.e. family, etc. must acknowledge to him/her that he/she is drug dependent. Not until such declaration is made can effective intervention be initiated. At this point, health care professionals can assist the drug dependent person in discovering the motives which caused his/her compulsive, non-controlled abusive drug taking behavior.

THE CLIENT

STAGE I

Denial is the first psychosocial trait stage seen before one admits to having a drug dependency problem. Denial is the refusal to believe or allow awareness of threatening or unpleasant aspects of external reality. The form denial takes varies from person to person, but can be characterized by the individual who says, "I don't drink any more than the next guy," "Doctor, I don't have a drug problem," "I can stop drinking anytime I want to," "You'd drink too if you had three teen-aged girls," "You would take drugs too if you had a job like mine," "My son is a good boy, he's not into drugs—that's for bad kids," or "Who in the hell do you think you are talking to me that way saying that I have a drug problem. I've seen you take a few drinks before." "It can't happen to me."

The use of denial prevents individuals from working toward recovery, i.e. the person is stuck and unable to move beyond this point. It also produces isolation, which turns into loneliness, a feeling which in turn produces increased drug-taking behavior. Thus, it becomes imperative that the family, friends, neighbors, and counselors become more involved with the drug dependent person in assisting him past this denial stage and move him onto recovery.

STAGE II

Esteem is the second stage which is concerned with feelings of personal self-worth. Self-worth is defined as a basic psychological feeling that all human beings possess in varying degrees. Among those who abuse drugs, this feeling is compromised or is not present at all. As a consequence, the person engages in self-abasement and reduced levels of functioning. This in turn leads to feelings of guilt and a continued escalation in abusive drug-taking behavior.

STAGE III

Confusion. The third stage is concerned with feelings of a chaotic and disorganized lifestyle now controlled by the demands of the drugs. It is here where the person begins to recognize the effects of an unordered drug life style with little or no regularity, (except for the drug experience) or predictability concerning normal every day life experiences. Thus, the person begins to ask, "Am I sick or just overworked," "Do I have a problem," or "I just need some medication to calm me down so that I can concentrate on my job."

STAGE IV

Loss of Significant Resources ("The Man With the Golden Arm") Syndrome is the fourth psychosocial trait seen before admitting to one's dependency on drugs and is often the first stage where recognition appears to occur. However, most drug abusers still do not perceive or want to deal with the effects, that continued abuse of alcohol or drugs may have on their lives. Consequently, they run a higher risk of going without assistance until they lose their most important possessions; e.g. job, family, health, home, finances and legal status. It is unfortunate that in the past some groups; i.e. psychologists and drug counselors, have assumed that a drug dependent person needed to hit rock bottom before he/she could be self motivated to enter and remain in treatment. Today, many professionals continue to at least limit their powers to motivate an individual to seek help early. The rationale for this is the belief that the person is solely responsible for his behavior and must be self-motivated to seek treatment. However, many believe that we can assist the drug dependent person to **declare** his dependency early by aggressive outreach or coercive approaches. Coercive techniques have been employed with some success by employers and unions through Employee Assistance Programs (EAP's). These techniques have also been used in the criminal justice system through the intoxicated driver of street crime programs to force the client into treatment with the threat of dire alternatives such as loss of job, jail and/or fines (Erfurt and Foote 1977; Pakull 1979). By imploring such techniques, we may be able to prevent the individual from losing significant resources in his/her life such as family relationships, friends, job, and health.

STAGE V

Acceptance is the stage where the drug abuser finally accepts his dependency on drugs by saying "I am drug dependent and I want to stop hurting—I need help." The acceptance of a drug problem signals the beginning of the search for treatment and eventual recovery from the ravages of the drug's effects. Once there is acceptance by the drug abuser, all community resources then may be mobilized to effectively assist the individual in acquiring medical, psychological, social, family, and legal assistance.

STAGE VI

Resolution is the sixth stage where the individual seeks a course of action, i.e., treatment to deal with his drug dependency. The form which resolution takes varies from person to person. For instance, the person may seek help by contacting a family physician for some health-related problem. Also, he may request assistance from the police, school counselor, employer, minister, by going to a crisis center, AA, or Al-Anon. Regardless of the means through which the drug abuser becomes involved in a treatment program, it is essential that a broad network of referral linkages exist between the drug program and other community resources.

STAGE VII

Entry is the final psychosocial trait in the process of declaring one's dependency on drugs. Treatment efforts are of little value if clients are not able to make the successful transition to independent drug free living. Thus, therapists should not only focus their efforts on providing adaptive learning and emotional skills, but also on insuring that the individual is prepared for the practical considerations involved in living a drug free life. Some practical considerations for re-entry into society may include the following: (1) acquiring a new set of drug free friends, (2) obtaining employment, (3) finding shelter, and (4) improving family relationships (See Table 8.0).

THE FAMILY SYSTEM

STAGE I

Denial. In the case of the family, the process of denial is similar. Within the family, members may deny the therapist's diagnosis and prognosis, or they may deny that the addict is an addict. Due to the highly charged emotions involved with the addict, certain family members will deny they are capable of controlling the situation or the addict. In this stage, psychological defenses are well established and the use of denial helps family members to maintain some level of self-esteem. The family's denial system acts as an enabler in the maintenance of his/her drug taking behavior. Thus, the family member(s) may explain the abusive drug taking behavior as being caused by some unknown psychological problem. Therefore, whenever the underlying etiology is discovered, the abusive drug taking behavior will cease, which implies that recreational usage of the drug can once again be practiced.

STAGE II

Esteem. In this stage, family members' self-worth is decreased and the family collectively feels self-pity because of their situation. This produces feelings of anger, resentment, anxiety, depression, and social isolation between the substance abuser and other members of the family.

Consequently, all attempts made by the family to control the situation result in failure, resulting in an increase of the drug taking behavior by the diseased member.

STAGE III

Confusion. During this stage, family members are confused and as a result work, social, school, and personal adjustment problems develop. Also, during this stage, there is an escalation of violence (e.g. child abuse, sexual abuse, spouse abuse) involving the entire family necessitating intervention by police, medical, and social services personnel. Consequently, the family feels alone, helpless, and trapped by their chaotic situation. These feelings thus cause the family to become immobilized to take any constructive action. In consequence, each family member develops some type of survival role to cope with an unbearable situation.

STAGE IV

Loss. During this stage, the family attempts to come to grips with the problems caused by the chemically dependent member. This is sometimes accomplished by exploring the possibility of a separation from the drug abusing member. In this situation, the family often feels torn between leaving and staying with the drug abusing member. This produces psychological isolation (e.g. drug abuser ignored by members of the family) from the diseased member thus creating guilt about desertion which in turn reinforces not taking any corrective action. Consequently, the family remains in a state of limbo over the pending loss of the drug dependent member (sometimes families may remain in this state forever). Whenever separation does occur, the family usually may not become a healthy system again. For example, new dependency or problems may develop in order to accommodate the new systems needs. There may be additional losses due to other family members leaving with the substance abuser. This of course places considerable financial stress on the remaining members. As a result, violence may increase whenever the substance abuser periodically returns for a visit.

STAGE V

Acceptance. During this stage, the family makes an adjustment around the problem thereby becoming less isolated. The family is now willing to accept the disability of chemical dependency and surrender their caretaker roles. At this point, family members are able to free themselves emotionally from the addict's problem and give ownership back to him/her. Once acceptance occurs, family members can care about the addict without caring for him/her. They are also free to understand him/her without taking on the problem should he/she return to their abusive drug taking behavior again. Furthermore, the family need not accept credit if the addict recovers.

STAGE VI

Resolution. During the resolution stage, the family may initiate aggressive drug treatment for the abuser or family if this is not possible. This initiation may be accomplished by getting the addict to trying AA, detoxification treatment, or by making an appointment with a drug therapist. During this stage, it is recognized that the entire family needs assistance to recover, as does the substance abuser.

STAGE VII

Entry. During this stage, the focus is on re-entering the family back into society as a healthy system; i.e. free from all those negative feelings seen in the above stages (See Table 8.0).

Table 8.0

PSYCHOSOCIAL STAGES FOUND IN D.E.C.L.A.R.E. THERAPY

Stages	*Psychosocial Issues and the Client*	*Psychosocial Issues and the Family*
1. Denial	Intellectualization, Displacement, Blocking, Avoidance, Isolation	Choreography, Dance around the problems (e.g. Waltz, Fast)
2. Esteem	Negativism, Selfbasement Inferiority, Incompetence	Immercement (Lack of Boundary Between Family and Client)
3. Confusion	"What's Happening to Me," "What's Wrong"	Unclear Boundary Due to Immersion at the Esteem Level
4. Loss of Resources	Job, Family, Friends, Health, Prosperity	Loss of Stability, Income, Survival for Living

Table 8.0 (*continued*)

Stages	Psychosocial Issues and the Client	Psychosocial Issues and the Family
5. Acceptance	"I am Dependent on Drugs"	Establishment of Clearly defined Boundaries (Vis-Vie-Ownership of Drug Problem), Use of Paradoxical Intention (Client is given Permission to Continue To Take Drugs; Consequences of Such Behavior is Clearly Defined).
6. Resolution	Seek Course of Action to Deal With Drug Dependency; i.e. Treatment	Treatment, for Family
7. Entry	Entry Back Into Society	Family Accepts the Drug Dependent Member Back into the Fold.

The whole process of acceptance, treatment, and entry back into society may be illustrated by the author's Drug Dependency Triad Configuration Hypothesis (Fig. 8.0). The "V" configuration represents or symbolizes victory over the bio-psycho-social effects of drug abuse which the author refers to as the "Churchill Syndrome." This simply means that the human spirit can prevail and triumph over the seemingly insurmountable odds of the drug(s) effects. Even with total disaster eminent, many drug dependent individuals can and have become victorious in the end much like the English were after the "Blitzkrieg" over London during World War II. However, what is needed is a strong aggressive, and collective effort on the part of the legal, social, and health care systems to assist the drug dependent person in combating his addiction.

In addition, the "V" depicts a sequence of important stages in the process of drug dependency. On the negative (descending slope) side of the "V" configuration are those stages which usually prevent successful intervention into the process of drug dependency. Thus, the descending slope represents the chronic self-destructive drug abuser who is without sufficient motivation to either accept or recognize the effects that contin-

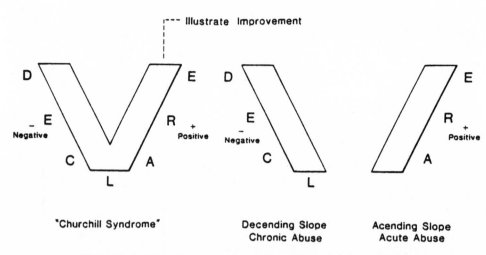

Figure 8.0. Drug dependency triad configuration hypothesis.

ued abusive drug taking behavior will have on his/her life. Consequently, drug abusers with a descending slope configuration run a greater risk of developing poor health, mental disturbances (e.g. psychosis) or possible death from prolonged drug abuse. Among those stages which inhibit successful intervention are denial, esteem, confusion and loss.

On the positive (ascending slope) side of the "V" configuration are found those traits which enhance the drug abusers chances of successfully recovering from the effects of drug dependency. The ascending slope thus symbolizes more of an acute form of drug abuse where the individual is highly motivated (by a variety of internal and external resources) to abstain from abusive drug-taking behavior. Individuals with this type configuration present a more hopeful picture for the health care system in its efforts to help the drug abuser.

The treatment of the substance disorder poses a unique set of variables not often seen with other types of clients. In consequence, it is vital that the counselor and client establish and maintain a positive interpersonal relationship. In addition, the counselor must develop a new set of positive attitudes toward the substance abuser. Negative attitudes though understandable are counterproductive and must not be allowed to enter the therapeutic process. All available evidence indicates that the larger population of substance abusers are responsive to intervention. In fact, modern companies having Employee Assistance Programs (EAP's) report that they are successful 70 percent of the time in treating the substance abuser.

Substance abusers, both young and old, respond quite well when counselors make an effort to learn and understand the abusers' life style. Once empathy, genuineness, openness and acceptance are communicated to the substance abuser, successful management can begin.

REFERENCES

Freud, S. *A General Introduction to Psychoanalysis*. New York: Permabooks, 1953. Boni & Liveright edition, 1924.

Herrnstein, R.J. The Evolution of Behaviorism. *American Psychologist*, 1977, 32, 593-602.

Kanfer, F.H., and Karoly, P. Self-Control: A Behavioristic Excursion into the Lion's Den. *Behavior Therapy*, 1972, 3, 398-416.

Pervin, L.A., *Personality: Theory, Assessment and Research*. New York: Wiley, 1980.

Spitzer, R.L., Klein, D.F., *Evaluation of Psychological Therapies*, 1976.

Szasz, T.S. *The Myth of Mental Illness*. New York: Harper, 1961.

Taylor, Janet A. Learning Theory and Personality. In J.M. Wepman and R.W. Heine (Eds.), *Concepts of Personality*. Chicago: Aldine, 1963. pp. 3-30. Technical recommendations for psychological tests and diagnostic techniques. Psychological Bulletin Supplement, 1954, 51, Part 2, 1-38.

Truax, C.B. Reinforcement and Nonreinforcement in Rogerian Psychotherapy. *Journal of Abnormal Psychology*, 1966, 71, 1-9.

Williams, J. *The Psychology of Women*, New York: Norton, 1976.

INDEX